MW01100683

Catch as Catch

*For David
in the reason page and
"stage rhyme"!*

CATCH AS CATCH

Robert Budde

TURNSTONE PRESS

Turnstone Press
607-100 Arthur Street
Winnipeg, Manitoba
Canada   R3B 1H3

Turnstone Press gratefully acknowledges the assistance of
the Canada Council and the Manitoba Arts Council.

Cover art: André Clément

Interior illustration: David A. Condie

Author photo: Debbie Keahey

Design: Manuela Dias

This book was printed and bound in Canada
by Hignell Printing for Turnstone Press.

Canadian Cataloguing in Publication Data

Budde, Robert, 1966-

Catch as catch

Poems.
ISBN 0-88801-185-7

I. Title.

PS8553.U43C3 1994   C811'.54   C94-920248-7
PR9199.3.B84C3   1994

to mom and dad, for taking me to Baytree
and the warm 6:00 a.m. milking barn where stories begin.

Acknowledgements

thanks to Dennis Cooley, inspiration and spirits, best-fiend
and demon with an editing pen, and Neil Besner who
showed me how to play it so I left myself shape on the eight.

thanks to Todd Bruce, who knows there is faith here too.

thanks to Robert Kroetsch and Dawne McCance for early
readings and revealing questions when the text didn't know
what it was asking.

and thanks to Debbie, for catching it all.

———————————————

aha!

(we said   together)

i caught you!

———————————————

Eli, Eli, lama sabachthani?

The Devil is the rebel of the cosmos, the independent in the empire of a tyrant, the opposition to uniformity, the dissonance in universal harmony, the exception to the rule, the particular in the universal, the unforeseen chance that breaks the law; he is the individualizing tendency, the craving for originality, which bodily upsets the ordinances of God that enforce a definite kind of conduct; he overturns the monotony that would permeate the cosmic spheres if every atom in unconscious righteousness and with pious obedience slavishly followed a generally prescribed course.
—Paul Carus

Accuse - v.t. To affirm another's guilt or unworth; most
            commonly as a justification of ourselves for
            having wronged him.
—Ambrose Bierce, *The Devil's Dictionary*

monday, may 3

*dark red fading to pink ear-lobes toes belly-button palms
soles of his feet he stood awkwardly and stilted a marionette with
loose skin and the chickens were pecking at his toenails furiously
the ragged edges fraying*

his eyes were yellow like ear wax

*he winced his lined face a twist the sky was cringing like
his scrunched nose thin his frame undernourished his belly
distended low so i gave him an apple from the pocket of my red wool
jacket it was only polite*

*the apple glinted extravagantly as it passed between our
hands*

*he accepted chuckling a thanks as he picked off the lint
broke the skin like punctured paper*

that was my first mistake

*i should have just ignored him as he slouched there his feet
shuffling in the dust taking an occasional kick at the insistent
chickens*

*but that's just it — here i was a simple man of flesh and
blood confronting — confronting what? — a ghost a myth a piece of
my imagination gone wild a pile of stories animated — it is the stuff
of legend but the pigs were anxious for their sugar beet tops and the
devil's eyes they propelled me*

*this is where it begins — a gesture plain and uncomplicated
(oh, why must we go on?) and his teeth were swallowed by the
white white apple flesh*

*i stood by him there on that infectious morning the apple
skin air snapped tight with sunlight cracking into pupils where we*

stood facing one another and i knew and he knew and that space
between us begged

    the void between us begged and we fell into conversation

    we had words

Anticipation

A beginning: the notion of extremes.

I would not have you know the devil. Leave him behind.
Take this back without apprehension. Yet lived.

The devil could easily walk away, off into a contorted
distance, this scrapbook under one arm. He talks back to us,
asking us to return him, call him home, take back my book.
Dispel.

Begin with something missed. Fallen out. Lost at the outset.
You began without me. Didn't miss me. You didn't catch my
fear – not until too late. My message slipped between the
cracks. Flammable.

Sometimes on a lazy spring morning an event occurs that
splits the sky open. A birthing, only slower. Reveals
distances. A dream it catches, spins emotions from nothing.
Catching your sleep-eyes it moves without impetus. Changes
the ways time folds about you. Changes the way space ticks
by you. This is the type of morning he wishes to describe to
you. Trick you into motion. Virtually. Staggered and still.

Disbelieve me. Exile me, you angel you.

A beginning: the past. Draw upon. Draw over. Clutter it up.

To do this thing would take a stranger. A strange element.
Almost sinister. With a wide-brimmed hat and a black sedan.
Windows tinted. He would have to be asking questions.
Looking for directions. Making notes. The sleepy little town
would have to find him foreign. Talk of him after he has left.
Remember small gestures, details, bits of conversation; the
way he glanced backward at odd moments, his tentative
fingers, the way he pronounced the word 'real.' He would
have to be looking for something, his eyes staring into

shadows behind the gas station, scanning the horizon, studying footprints, signs of fire. Someone. Searching. Almost desperate.

A beginning: the spring. The morning clear full. Sound of flies' wings against the air. The space between audible. Purple eyes in dung.

He would plant a crop for you to gather in your arms the fruit spilling between your fingers over your tongue. Preserving for winter. Snow intuition.

Momentum. Beginning a scrapbook – floppy and dear. Momentum – moving beneath your fingers.

Begins again: don't look back. Even when you feel him watching don't look back.

Doubt me. Who is speaking.

Salvation is just another word for servitude. Release me.

A beginning: sewing thread will never kink if you always make your knot in the end of the strand that leaves the spool first. A revolution. Lick the frayed end, thread through, the eye of a needle, full. Meet me there.

Begin an end already – the sound suspended. Waiting to begin.

A meeting place over words. Reconsidered afterwards. Pick it up. Keep it from me, a secret. A secret scrapbook held close, too close, it begins to fall apart.

Something falls out.

A beginning: a memento. A matchbook from the Blue & Gold falls, catches your eye. A flick of wrist and it is caught. Held up to the last little bit of light. Maybe a rough sketch of a demon on the inside. Maybe one match missing. A boy looking a little frightened. The chance of ignition, firestorm.

aha! Catch.

Hand it back.

farm hazards: obscure

the sense of accusation: (see also self-depreciation) the way
   the furrowed dirt that kicks up in small bowls of dust
   around your boots mirrors your grimy secrets,
   reconstructs your lust; in roadside ditches, scattered
   outcrops of stone, the neighbour's kitchen; your rage in
   the frilled sticky rows of oats now beginning to lie down
   under the weight of their dangerously inbred heads; the
   violence of fences – barbed wire across eye; the insecurity
   of dugouts filled with runoff, the distance between
   sources; sheds left from the failed pheasant project; you
   relent. for prevention; dig into the roots of alfalfa the tiny
   tendrils of timothy stalks, rub them into your skin; walk
   naked with the holsteins; take down fences around the
   cash crops; pull the fields into irregular shapes, have
   them dive into the woods; collect pin cherries, wild
   strawberries, hazelnuts, green onions, sage, whitecaps,
   red clover flowers, rose-hips, recipes, irregular potions,
   make dandelion wine; take a week and wander off your
   land, show people your scars, have them show theirs.
the auger: for the maintenance of order between point A and
   B; the churning of motion through a narrow space; built
   to screw up; chewing swallowing spitting– it will take
   apart stretch you out begin with a stray bit of you – a
   scarf to prevent a chest cold, a leather belt with rearing
   horses on the buckle, a shoe lace left unbound, tattered
   edges, curious fingers, a misplaced kick, an adventurous
   tongue. for prevention; work naked; don't reveal
   protuberances; conceal thyself.
the couple: for the maintenance of order between point A and
   B; naked to the stark revolution of sun; many conflicts
   occur over misguided paths; the keen edge of difference
   sounding in the morning conversation – the curt call of a
   baltimore oriole egging them on; the division of chores –
   habit, routine; the silence between words we fill in like
   old fences; absent commandments. for prevention;
   cross-dress; invite the devil over; show each other your

scars; walk naked with the herd; reveal protuberances; have sex at inconvenient times.

the combine: for the separation of grains from chafe and straw – the tailings and loose ends; accomplishes this through a violent shaking that dislodges and loosens the grain from the cut stalk; picks up the swathes with a belt of metal tines; a sharp pickup line; the soul and body shook free; a truck is often driven alongside the combine to shuttle the grain straight from the combine to a granary – many conflicts stem from the misguided paths of truck and/or combine; dust may also accumulate and spontaneous combustion is a danger. for prevention; you are one with the machine; don't move ahead of yourself; use the tailings as bedding, mulch, insulation, worth is not relative; invite a stranger to sit in the cab of the combine with you; with you.

the plow: for turning over soil; breaking up, breaking in; furrows occur; to keep land from becoming impenetrable; to prepare for a planting; danger of digging too deep and revealing artifacts; hitting stony frowns; the remote danger of freezing to death.

the neighbour: (see also, the feud) in close proximity. common dangers most often relate to property and/or party lines; results in frosty corrugated conversations for one's tongue to get stuck on, stern fences, spontaneous combustion, the sense of accusation. for prevention; loop the lines make them uncertain use fake voices have the devil hired as telephone operator; hold square dances that career off the floor into mud into heaven; talk politics; show each other your combines; admire each other's choice of baler twine, feel the texture of their's first; never talk over fences; set rhubarb pie on back steps on cloudy mornings; fix machinery together; make your conversations irregular shapes – dive them into woods.

the baler: for forming hay or straw into neat bound bales – either rectangular or large round ones; able to package someone into a suitcase in seconds; conformity for easy stacking – heaven is a cozy loft; stooking for

watershedding ability – the interrogation of rain. for
prevention; appreciate your extremities; don't get roped
in to systems; walk in the rain with the holsteins;
appreciate the singular.

the succession: for the continuance of the male bloodline and
the retention of family property/name; involves hearty
back-slapping, schizophrenia, mysterious deaths,
macrame; daughters who walk softly their feet not
touching the earth; worth is relative; the insecurity of
brome grass, timothy, alfalfa, bibles, almanacs, cream
separators, the way you hesitate before turning down the
gravel road to home; lazing around dugouts thinking of
runoff with you. for prevention; search for the well of
eternal you without success; hire an heir; collect money
for not planting this year; mechanize to extremes, the
pompous pistons and gears will explode your
vocabulary; ask daughters to take up beekeeping,
pheasant farming, whatever you have failed at; mix
bloodlines until they cease; loop.

the devil: for the possibilities; provides safety tips of all types
when you are feeling the most secure; digs to the roots, to
the pulp, to the sweet, juicy, grade A bits (his face and
nails covered in mud and hell is not so far away now);
celebrates schizophrenia nearly twice as much as you do;
bakes a divine rhubarb pie; will deceive you of your
deceptions; has no heir and very little hair; may cause
anything in irregular shapes, at odd times, when the
weather presumes different (and you praying for rain).
for prevention; show him your scars – don't ask to see
his; sing with him a song much like that of the baltimore
oriole on a day when he doesn't wish to sing but, of
course, must; with you as one with

Devil   Demiurge   Teufel

Ganesha   Sakla   Dagon

Mammon   Moloch   Apolyon

Beast   Tempter   Belial

Urita   Archfiend

Dragon   Lucifer

Lightbearer   Azazel Prince of Darkness   Lilith

Loki   Spirit that Denies   Diabolus

Set   Ahriman   Rimmon   Satan

Errour   Rogue   Angel   Asmodeus   Hecate

Shadow   Fallen One

Phlegethon   the Other   Thoth

Mephistopheles   Demon   Eblis Serpent

Hoberdidance   Apostate   Pluto

Damian   Sammael   Semihazah

Astaroth   Trickster   Typhon   Omniarch

Pan   Jupiter   Screwtape

mKha'sGroma   Prince of Matter   Mastema

Lord of Underworld   Antichrist

Beelzebub   Black Archangel   Lucy   Evil One

Nicholas   Huwawa   Leviathan   Behemoth

Old Horny   Dis   Hades

Wild Huntsman   Saturn   Lagartianick

Windigo   Black Bogey   Jack   Brendly   Okee

Tiamat   Enoch   the Eternal Malcontent

11

                    caught
        a crack   clasp
        hung out   the release a descent
                              breaking up
        a split
                running between your feet
                        found me   falling
        apart   fragile i was
          struck   decked   bowled over
                due   to a speech   high pitch
                    the glass splinter
              tinkle of me (glint did you see)
              parted my ways   cast me
                              a side   broke
        my will
                        i was soundly bedeviled
            uncomposed
i will never get it
                                        together again
                written off

(catch it before it hits
                                    home)
                a piece   a soul
                            souvenir

              moved me this way
              and an other
                    you you you
              made me
                    many

(detail: Abraham Rattner, *Place of Darkness*, 1947. Oil on canvas.)

              bare leered
                            rude & shining like misuse
           the exhibitionist flayed
                            inhibitions you held off
                 the thin edge crude and
                    slick he gypped you of pretense
                                   cracked the buttons
                                        plummeted difference
              closed the steps between
                            collision and hindsight
                 design carried like a flashlight
                            the beige trenchcoat of desire
           backlit   to shudder senses
       turn a phrase
                            of moon

dangle

                            and you say
                      i don't hear you listen

with	a hint of hesitation
with	out motive
with	a chance of blowing snow. into swirling intuition, the music of insulation
with	an assumed identity, another name, without knowing
with	a sad harbinger of words a careful singer squeezed voice trained and mute he lolls his tongue whines his meaning his lack of a mean streak will you listen to his late-night bladder lament
with	growing disdain you leave the audience find a tv linger on the curl of pretzel
with	out hope for recovery the machines grow wings flap behind your eyelids
with	a fear of witches you seek healing the stakes high search her out open your fever to her touch
with	love
out	of nothing
with	words
out	of grace cast from deposed (the silver-lined ones hurling insults
with	heaven filled with that silvery light and no shadows there was no use for a third dimension no need for depth no cause for inside behind undercover – only up/down left/right. love was the sound of two pages falling together. outside of bodies we find a sense in disorder. foreign. the way a car veers into a crowd kills four not five. the way a comet falls on a road where a couple stood the night before. wishing. The neat flow-chart of life the square elements versus the tumble of surfaces textures

	the clash of cymbals. the irregular rhythm of

the clash of cymbals. the irregular rhythm of
heartbeats versus the rattle of the speed of sound
the lurch of time zones the snap away
from 4/4
with   a warped sort of warmth we order the world into
skins, huddle into ourselves, your body a hot
thought across the campfire sparks
out   of bounds
with   gamesmanship, c'mon buddy gogogoggggo hudda
buddy shoot shoot whoop it up
out the window i jumped overboard
with   you   (now that's a lie)
out   witted, i would steal your ears hold them dear and
you wondering where to hook your glasses
with   an ungainly voice (gaps stops misplaced breaths
cracks flat sharp a gasp of recognition or
something like it just out of tune always loud)
the most appealing song may be sent to your ears.
the thump and swish of snow angels. wet bums.
dream us. out.

there is no evil
nothing has prepared you for this has it, preacher
wrap your tongue around it
do not let it fall
evil is fear made other
unmake it with me

resist the temptation to fall silent
and say it again

there is no evil

saturday, may 17

spring in this region comes quick the black loam soil releases water as insistently as the black rolling clouds. water vibrates in the mournful gloom. and every spring we lost the outhouse. not stolen, although it had suffered that indignity often enough, but lost into the very bowels of the earth. water comes burping and giggling down from the hills and pastures in an exalted pilgrimage of rivulets, streams, flows, torrents, and gushes. chores become an aquatic adventure and, once again, we lose the outhouse. the unhappy mansion begins to lean and shudder as the soil of its foundation turns uncertain. irrevocably it begins to slide into the hole. trips into it become tenuous dances with disaster, the enigmatic throne prone to lurches and groans, no longer do the comics taped to the wall or stacks of mags comfort, no longer does the neat crescent moon cut into the door console. every moment potential apocalypse.

every year we try to prevent the inevitable. the hired help, the Chisums, Michael and Lil Fletcher from across the creek, old man Bently, Rob Calvin from town – we rig up the horses. judge leverage, balance. prepare for battle. Ken strokes his chin. the two brothers from Nepena roll up their sleeves take quick glances at Mrs. Fletcher who is checking the horses' bits. we steel ourselves. dig our heels in. begin to try to pull the beloved structure from its doom. one of the Chisum kids eats green grapes off to the side of the horses where she sits cross-legged in the short feathery fox-tails. she laughs at her three brothers as they posture and strut. the outhouse is on the brink. just as the depths beckon beyond resistance, just as the sulfurous chasm threatens to engulf we strap ourselves in and rage against the treachery of gravity.

PULL! C'MON PULL HARD!

the devil stands behind us his hand on his forehead – "must you with that infernal racket – preacher man, if you're going to shout so at least have the decency to swear a little." but he is transfixed. awed by our valiance.

16

C'MON PULL! PULL HARD! HYAW ROBBER! PULL!

*we sweat grunt strain coax plead. the exertion distorts our
vision sends stars and swirls into our sight like after-images. men
and women, young and old bend and fold into the effort. Ken's
overalls tear. someone loses a boot. the ground churns.*

NICK! PULL! PULL HARD!

the devil, he joins us.

*in the rain we become one with the outhouse. the mud
covering us sucks at out intentions. threatens to bury us choke us
fill our noses ear mouths. blurs our features.*

C'MON PULL – GODDAMMIT! PULL HARD!

*we lose, we are loose. the sky collapses in. we slide into the
earth. fall spinning into the infinity of soil. the abyss claims us.
mud and clay cling. rope wood flesh tangles. splinters. and then the
splashes of shame. confused knots of defeat. jostles of flesh. lumps of
hands and a stray caress. and out of the descent and chaos comes
the clear wet release into laughter and foulness. shit, we all say.
shit, it's noisy. shit it's warm. we find each other feeling our way
through the darkness and the dank earth. our voices boom names.
swear. hand in hand we ponder our next move.*

the out

house

away we
went

in con
trol

alone with
ours
elves

wet gobbling
breath

and the dark re
cesses

the imagined
nip

at our nakedness

he named me
he named me pervert
            castrated me
named me outlaw
            nailed me to a tree
            paper thin
named me criminal
            jailed me, refused bail
            fed me lines
named me deviant
            punished me with relish
named me lover
            distorted, made me huge
named me ambitious
            beat me to the punch
named me foreign
            dubbed me badly
named me thief
            stole my hands
named me disobedient
            assumed power
named me violent
            threw me from a great height
named me powerful
            named me devil
named me opposite
            bound me
            mirror, mirror on the wall . . .
named me articulate
            forked my tongue
named me witch
            burned me
named me political
            slandered me, pulled the platform
            from beneath my feet

named me sexual
            watched me move
named me cruel
            flayed the skin from my back
named me learned
            read of me
named me beautiful
            broke my wings
            (my lovely wings)
he named me rebel
            denied me
he named me
            son

He broke the horizon with a wake of dust and exhaust. The line between brilliant blue and the dun earth broken, turned ragged, revealed distances. A raging headlong nothing that transfixed the handful of townspeople who saw its approach. Beneath the cloud, winking mirrors and dazzling flashes of sunlight snagged more eyes. He lingered, hinged on the horizon. Like this he appeared to Baytree. Chrome and smoke. Quiet infamy. Evidence.

He pulled into the Blue & Gold for gas, tucking his smooth-lined sedan between Scoop's half-ton and a yellow grader, the driver snoozing in the cab. He stood uncertain for a moment – half expecting someone to come out to fill it up for him. He worked the old pump as if it were an angry dog. It rumbled and wheezed. His jacket whipped around him brushing the ground. In the metal corrugated building he paid the young Horner boy at the till. He asked some questions leaning over the counter into the boy's replies. They both pointed in several different directions – the stranger in an uncertain conformation of the landscape, questioning the map the young boy unfolded in his replies. Coulee, bluff, pasture-lease, back-quarter – Baytree entered his imagination. He pulled out several folded pieces of paper and set them on the counter so that they faced the boy. Squinting the boy shrugged his shoulders a few times, holding is hands outward, a little frightened. He handed the papers back to the stranger. The stranger became visibly upset, gave the boy a bill, took a pack of matches, left.

Later, the boy told us that his name was Chorus and he was looking for the devil. He had heard a rumour. And now he was here, looking. He could feel the hot gravel road through the soles of his shoes.

At his car door he stood a minute peering at the roads. He looked at the sun and decided on directions. Began.

Appearances: Photo #4

an intense young monk, or advisor, or prince hiding a keen dirk beneath splendiferous robes the setting is eons ago baroque at the very least he garbles distorts the lighting it is difficult to see his face looking like gold

Catch stands washing a saucepan while I dry. I watch her move, looking for thunder. She tells me about Jay and El, and Apology. She pauses on small details while she adds more hot water, dries her hands, jumps ahead excited and plunges her hands into the water again. She usually returns to Jay after straying, speaking of him with a tenderness that made a mystery of such a simple man. She walks through his ritual chores, sorts through his endearing orderliness, mimics his stuttered phrases. She calls him uncle, but her voice makes uncle something magic, still close and alive. She talks of that first blustery morning when Jay met the devil as if she was there, studying their awkward dialogue. I know she has never met the devil, she told me that straight out with obvious regret, but as she speaks through the lives of the three, their voices carry word of his presence. His escapades drift in through the eyes and mouths of those she trusted most. Especially her mother. Apology's love affair with the devil fascinates her, she lingers on it, frames it, returns to it often. While she speaks, washing, she uses her little finger to pull her long red hair from her face when strands stick to her lip or hide her eyes.

i am something from nothing. life from mud stacked with electric love vibrating me free. i took my first breath from the exhalation of my name in a lost angel's anger he planted a seed of me whispering his own freedom. i first stole air. lips close. forget me not father.

i am the beginnings the stray chance off beat fall into a gorgeous mistake. the blues, wrapped in red and afraid.

i am spontaneous combustion the burst of infamy. the tailings and dust accumulating past a pressure point the spaces between particles become volatile no spark necessary the elevator trembling from within. grain dust a phoenix rising. your lungs set to explode. energy where none was before sourceless and essential.

i am masturbation the flailing spew from the strobe of the mind. i am repetitions again and again i will fall for you. i am memory embedded in memory.

i am abstract as an awkward simile placed peculiar. i am the leap the tangent impetus the jumped rail i am syntax made strange once in i am fluid drink of me.

i am immediate. i am the breaker the crest the brink the point of no cracking. i am the harbinger of storm, harboured hard and stark. shelter, there is here, a softer shelter. melt with me, my words.

i am an authentic forgery untraceable the perfect stroke of ink across vintage white. let me let me let me steal your attention. penmanship is everything.

i am vagabond fears imprinted textured by many hands. grip.

i am the contact precise at the receiving tip of nerves balanced between momentum and reaction. skin twitch.

i am the inhalation before words are arranged flung with a bit of spit.

i am a book that maps the fine threads of your fears. their colourful disguises.

i am becoming iambic coming. i am taut thrumming.

i am dying.

i am read, whited-out, blackened and blue for you.

i am the verge of shorelessness.

i am the sweaty gap between fabric and skin the undertone of manners. i am the fascination of mirrors your own image the play between and back you pose eyes following the path of eyes. i am obsession the piss-up kicking the props from propriety. i am the history of shame. i am shadow. the leftovers of light that eats up incongruity. i am shelter, pull the cover over, close. go naked in the rain. I am tired.

i am the anger of desecration revelry the chaos of rolling bodies the orgies of unrestraint the acting out of the forbidden. i am all that is unknown all that is beyond reason a wizard's stock of spells the witches' coven the cannibal's hunger the maniac his beautiful brokendown dance. i am the celebration of deviance.

i am the announcement of bodily function fuck no the turn the articulation into touch and taste into words hitting sharp accents shit piss come cunt prick cock juice yes. and wrap your tongue around this.

i am those that back us, back us into excessive am i that succubus you beseech.

i am petulance a young lover's challenge hips thrust forward lips parted soundless. i am the way a muscle will clench twitch an adrenalin rush reflex catch me snap. i am the chase willy-nilly sporadic inconclusive in dust and wreckage. i am inconsistent jazz and bourbon the arrival of climax unexpected the ecstasy landing where it will.

i am jagged shimmering inner surfaces split me open. i am the vertigo of deception of precarious distance the dizzying laughter stunning the magic involutary.

i am a secret. i am a secret tucked away, tucked away in a secret place, told to a secret person. ssshhhhhhhhh.

i am not a pipe. look close at my frames and struts, my pencil strokes and shades, my floodlights and facades. try to touch me to your lips. puff.

i am contradiction. i am your eyes when you must steal. i am insurgence the swarming words defiant motioning and intervening. i am procession.

i am plural except for once a long time ago.

i am insecure footing teetering. i am run on galloping frenzied i am horizon kissed by an unforgiving sun i am mythology sprung loose tactile i am rubbing against your leg tingling on your tongue brushing against your active fingertips ecstatic i am spoken flesh in a wise woman's vocal chord i am heavenly i am the devil

seeing
a way

of seeing

    if you catch him standing still against the stark
backdrop of trees, sky or white of memory
    if he doesn't realize your gaze
    if you stand still for hours studying
    if you look close at the play of light across his frame,
the white of his turned eyes, the shallow curves and tensions
under his skin
    if you watch long enough his absent motions his
unconcerned humming his distracted shuffling
    if you were this focused you would be obsessed

wouldn't you

look away

actor actor

the lines looped about his neck singing

the black background blends in

stilted and teetering, just barely

his tight disguise shimmered like an unlikely metaphor

or like heat

the front row aghast & upright, the mirror they hung

wavering   then turn, his internment over

the intermission beheld the frenzy

voices   the soundtrack continues off-cue

the stage deflated   collapsed into milling   positions

please please

over the intercom you spoke your absence

you abduct, rapt

sure of an encore, a scenic seizure with

the theatre folded in

closed unrehearsed

except for a furtive curtain call

by me   just by me

cloth, whispers of a gap

–why do you call me preacher, anyway? you know by now i'm as religious as a hungry hog in heat. i'm just a guy, all i do is farm. i don't think i preach to anyone, i don't talk that much. on top of that i don't much like those . . . those . . . type of men.

–do you mean men of the cloth or killers who like to wear strings of their victims' teeth?

–no . . . i mean, you know, ministers or pastors or priests, i never know which. i'm nothing like one of those. so, why do you call me that name?

–i know no other.

–Jay, my name is Jay.

–J or Jay?

–i don't see the difference.

–it's such an empty name, it has no weight like stan, or caesar, or richard, robert, lear, michael, jesus, christopher, saviour, destruction, rampant, idol, pleasure, or even hey, hey, you. how should i call you nothing. it would be like touching through glass. it must be exciting, though, i guess. like being naked in the rain. i wish you would name me. i mean, how should you call me. you should . . . knit me a new name, preacher. make it a net and sing for a catch of silver starlight.

tuesday, june 13

*a late-lurking frost killed the zucchini, the devil broke the
news with a smirk;*

*—our zucchini plants are all brown and definitely dead, i
think (the devil hates zucchini)*

*—that's impossible, zucchini plants never die, they survive
anything, even if you try to kill them they still grow and grow, even
if you don't want them to (i guess i broke down a little at this point)
you mean to tell me that we can't even grow zucchinis right, that
we can't even grow fucking zucchinis, not even FUCKING
ZUCCHINIS!!*

*the devil touched my rough fingertips, took my shoulder,
led me to the seed box he said anger is healing, brussel sprouts
planted in silence on a heavy August afternoon. knots of guilt
tucked into furrows, rolling green in January.*

"Idleness – n. A model farm
where the devil experiments
with seeds of new sins and
promotes the growth of staple
vices."
—Ambrose Bierce,*The Devil's
Dictionary*

30

only in Apology's house
        do the paintings make love

they shudder and tug free
            their frames left gangly
            pompous even the neat angles &
    hook left hanging

the paintings flop like lop ears
    they edge closer edges eager to overlap

the curl & rumple & ever so careful
        roll onto the carpet &
        there they are
    the sudden corner petting skyline
            looking for the ridge of horizon

it doesn't matter: oil or acrylic
        a light stipple snag in long strokes
    or a wash of sandy dun
they touch always manage to touch
        colours lick and converge
        verging on vermillion
    olive on blue-grey or burgundy
        auburn on flagrant
                pink they burst

& the sound of that canvas ampersand
    the desperate arch into one another
    arcing to folded figure eights
    they perform a symphony of purple sound
        the dry rasp & crimp
        the crumpled whisper of love

wisp & fold wisp & fold wisp & fold wisp wisp wisp wisp

intake breath
wild rose just before a stroke
            slipped onto the frame
   and you turned
                brush poised

      saw his face
            pressed against the window

      his gaze

               dripping

my name
apology
entertaining the devil
my name
amusing him

apology
he says the word
over
an anthem

he asked me to portrait him
like they had always done
stroke the brazen lash of mouth
cringe his face red and black
the shadows writhing
snarl the textures

he assumed a pose
put on a growl

but i cannot paint evil

instead i will paint his pain
dark red bending to pink

pretend
shadows
are your own
watch them in
terpret
your dance let them
enter
tain

turn

our dark
to dusk

33

thursday, june 19

so the devil was in love. that summer she could have him do
anything. he seemed always present. always everywhere. every
minute of her day. just shy of becoming a nuisance or aggravating.
she made him anxious, aware of his own colour. she called him a
fascist and she was right. he made her laugh. spent hours crooked
on a saw-horse watching her hand as it spread touched glided
smudged feathered washed the paint onto canvas. he cooked broccoli
and asparagus for her – spoke poems to her while she slept – wove
wild swirling rugs for her to walk dizzy on – rubbed against her
moans as he massaged her back – played cards with her late into the
night when she needed sleep – begged her not to send him away. she
smiled at his antics unafraid to call him silly or ignore him. she
often forgot he was there perched on a saw-horse his eyes holding
her painting like a glimpse. he embraced her rejection. her disdain.
her distance like a lover unto itself. he quivered with delight when
she stared through him not seeing. he gaped in awe when she left
walking down the driveway without a look back . he leapt into the
air with empty glee when she said she didn't love him. she ripped
up the poems he wrote, tore the unread words and shoved them into
her mouth, swallowing while he watched. she threw a bottle of ink
at him, just missing. but she picked him up when he tripped under
her cool gaze. she fed him when he forgot to eat. one night she
dressed him in the dozens of costumes she had tucked in her attic
chests and drawers. he became a purple bunny an army captain a
pirate complete with bug-eyed parrot on one shoulder an
executioner a fireman a frankenstein an angel with a wand of
sparkles and ballet slippers. a pumpkin although the paper mache
split spilling him onto the floor. a dracula a gorilla. a devil. when he
posed with the plastic horns, a wired rubber tail and a flimsy
diabolical grin they both collapsed laughing hard enough they

thought their sides would split, rolling on the rug until tears
trickled free. they hugged and she bit his lip, licked his nose.

her name he found was Apology. and the devil, he was
sorely tempted.

"You will rejoice to hear that no
disaster has accompanied the
commencement of an
enterprise which you have
regarded with such evil
forebodings."
—Mary Shelley

Places the apology and the devil were caught playing dirty:

1) late one hot June night on the very top of the Blue & Gold diesel holding tanks, their lovemaking explosive and purple

2) in the crook of an apple tree, straddling branches with the sleeping robins, they talked about relatives in the morning glow; now that's a lie

3) on a combine, in the cab curled around the stick-shift and in the holding bin, grain dust spilling over them like mice

4) at centre ice, oblivious to the chipping away, to the whistled offside, to the yawning goals at either end, to the teams that waited along the boards to drop the puck

5) in Jay's barn, the cows not at all concerned by their thrashing and laughter

6) in god's bedroom once they snuck, late in the middle of forever, they stole in, dove under the endless covers, they left the stains, the disheveled linen, the lingering smell of desire opened up

7) in a canoe, lapping the shore with their love, over and over, the waves touched sand and then back out again

8) in aisle eight of tomboy grocery, on piles of bakery goods, cellophane squeaking, they left the crumbs out for the birds

9) on the rim of the rimrocks, teetering, limbs dangled over into air, they made the stone warm, then hot, liquid beneath their love-making, all five horizons revolved, fell into them, this was the last time

ow, baby
i'm burnin
burnin up for you
my heart is on fire it's a flame
c'mon light me up
i'm hot for you can'tcha see
honey you gotta do it to me
flick my switch, turn me on
burn me from both ends
youze gotta stoke my stove
feed my flame til i inferno
i'm the spark for yer pilot light
darlin let's set the night on fire
i'm on my knees baby jus beggin
let's blow this place sky high
burn under them bridges forget bout crossin
oh baby i'm sendin you a flare an sos
so as we can red-line it
fire it up, rev my engine
hotter'n a frog on a hot rock
let's make some fireworks fly
heat things up, raise a little hell
jus you an me, jus us baby
let's stay in that there hot ol kitchen
c'mon baby i'm beggin, i'm pleadin
i'm burnin' up, sizzlin
i'm holdin a torch for ya
i'm losin it, straight losin it
you gotta wet my desire honey
cool me off, pull my plug, pull it
let me dive into yer water
drown in yer love
you gotta douse me girl
you gotta douse me now

fire (fir) n. – a chemical reaction, the burning of a combustible substance with oxygen that releases heat and light; great enthusiasm, fervour, passion, verve, fury; rapturous abandon; seizure, fit; v. – raise the emotions of, set off; to project or throw suddenly and forcefully; to bake in a kiln ('fire' an urn); to leave embers, ashes, cinders.

> the indistinct edges of flame
> dissolving into air

(love and anger might be all i'm trying to get to . . . yes, love and anger, and maybe regret . . . and urgency, i would like to convey urgency – the rush of love short on time)

Ya, i said he could stay but only as long as he didn't whine or leave socks lying around. I'm not a maid and i'll never be anybody's 'girlfriend.' I got no patience for that kind of shit. I told him so, too. I just like sex, plain and simple. It's healthy. Real and good. So what if i'm damned to hell. Wouldn't be the first time now, would it. Jesus, if hell has sex like this, count me in. I'll bet there's no sex in heaven. I'll just bet. No good sex at least. Stiff upper lip sort of sex, quick and clean. No thank you. Our first night though, he was sure scared. I though maybe it's modesty or he was catholic or something but man, no, it wasn't that. It wasn't that at all. Ya see, the guy has no dick. Never thought i'd see the day. I reached and almost fell out of bed, like leaning on a wall that's not here or something, you know what i mean. Like anarchy it was. There's just this hard warm crotch and it twitches under my fingers. I was cool about it, anyway. Just kept on like everything was peachy. It was kind of exciting is what it comes down to. I never come much fucking anyway. The other stuff, touching, rubbing, licking, that stuff was what i really got off on. He didn't know how to do that much either, but we had nothing else to do, so i showed him. He learned quick. Whooooeeee, think i'll keep him. What the hell. He said he loves making love upside-down. Not like me on top but really upside down, feet in the air or tied from a beam or something I don't know. But i think i'll keep him. Hell, it can't be that bad, now can it.

Appearances: Photo #6
        missing. destroyed in a 1979 fire. though remains were never recovered, foul play was never considered. ashes to ashes.

monday, may 3

    dark red fading to pink palms ear-lobes nipples she stood.
sudden. brazen. took me by surprise her body sucking at my eyes.
crimson. she gazed at my thighs forearms neck took me close began
to remove my work-clothes undid my collar took my boots tossing
them aside. i stood still, stunned by suppleness. her motion and my
own nakedness. my skin glaring white my hair, my feet and hands
floppy my cock uncertain. defensive.

    she folded me to the grass with a quick motion against the
back of my knees. lowered me down my fall with her heavy arms.
began to kiss my skin chest neck belly. her hair surrounding.
clothing me. the clover beneath a wet intake of breath. she began
again. my hands found the point where her tail met the rest of her
spine. it thrashed. and again. her tongue feathered around mine.
flicked at my ear. she coiled above striking the yellow sky with her
red. and.

    there were no words. no temptation to explain. resist.

    and began again.

    the sun flew over and moon and then again.

    seized.

    she was immediate. i was right after that.

    again.

any guilt of longing brushed aside making your
reluctance skip lose balance mix citrus with the smooth of
poplar bark with the breath of an iris deep and dark the
shock of water lapping against warm belly. your senses
would pant at the loss of punctuation tongue feeling edges
ears tasting eyelids listening to the hum of skin his love
would be like bulrushes bursting soft-white in your nose
breathing underwater the sun spangled and spliced by the
ripples your words said his love would be a pine cone
startling between your fingers nicking your palm an ecstatic
whisper of desire deep in its falling the lushness of wet lichen
against your thighs a host of monarch butterflies against
your eyelids terror on the wings of the very next stroke of
frantic orange and he would touch you exactly where you
least expect and most desire your body coaxed alive the
wonderful variables of undress and cooing he would slowly
empty the space between you and the intimate just now
teasing the sparrow into your palm and planting his secrets
in his silence and he crouches as if hiding in a stealth of
fiddleheads and columbine the sun ambling the mossy pine
trunks hushed the swallows and flickers propelled by the
shade and there is blackberry juice dribbling down your chin
the world stippled and buzzing with blue he walks naked
with you breathing your body's scent you almost ashamed at
your brash rush through scrub brush you stop linger over
clover you hover over bluebells and bleeding hearts like bees
the tingling skin of his neck until the ground becomes the
paths of your skin traced across cheek neck shoulder down
risk of chest jump of nipple singing across your belly the
warm moist mingling and that tree with the long low
branches that tree there would be wonderful to tumble under

i know
i know

the devil tends flowers
at home in a damp release from loam

simple message
made flesh
colours rolling wide
aromatic a slope
edges beckoning

sing to me azure &
i may love you

breezeblown
to catch a fading twilight
reflects and collects
the incandescence all
told through petal and pistil
and perfumed surfaces
powdered runs and curls
glowing seams and
a pouting flourish

butterfly me
my sound tickled stamen

the dazzling passage of seed

were you lost
where words are in the dark
saying love, read to me
it is the night the late
it is dark but not the dark
that breaks and seethes
but a dark i know you
can see i know
& in this dark that you
hold i wait a slight
weight in your hands
it is dark & my pages
tremble my cover worn
and frayed you feel
my binding split tongue
your finger over my imperfect
edges the places where
others have scribbled
themselves between my lines you
breathe but my words
that blur in the dark the ink
leaping from pages eyes
dilated tease armless i wait
touching my aimless turn my
voiceless signs waiting you hold
my tongue through space
in silence i hear your breath
pleat my fold you hold please
let you speak my darkness open
to your hands your skin brush
traces my thin darkness draped
in corners edges my margins wait
for your release your hands
hold this breath in the waiting
dark i wait to hear
you voice me

43

the moth invented the flame
drew its flicker in
breathing its perfume
wings like lungs

the moth invented the flame
became brush to paint shadows
a lover darting huge
the ceiling, walls of possibility

the moth invented the flame
to distort the terrifying blue
the rows of clean white birch
the screen gleams like teeth

the moth invented the flame
and a leaping cocoon dream
candlestick wax wrapped
melting into a nimble tip

the moth invented the flame
like a lily from heaven
its curves and sweet sanctum
divulged, incense and ash

the moth invented the flame
to mock the butterfly glamour
the monarch so virtuous and clean
their hidden orgies the inferno

the moth invented the flame
to end the story
with dazzle and flare
and a tense lingering smell

a scent you still remember
every time you fall in love

monday, may 3

   dark red fading to pink fingertips palms earlobes wrists
soles of his feet he startled me from my solitude. with a wry grin he
beckoned me come nearer. pssst, he said, hey, over here. i watched
his eyes his tall swooping frame the morning light pooling around
him the chickens gathered at his feet like sheep. flies hummed an
anthem around us. his exotic fragrance the sound of his poise his
clothing his long crooked finger.

   we had words.

   flourishing a thick paisley cape he walked in front speaking
of betrayal. of unjust exile, a nasty eternity in a filthy country full
of squat harsh-tongued peasants. he talked freedom and pleasure. of
dreams, like you, he crooned his smile glistened and i felt him read
my thoughts, his immaculate hands fingering the new-smelling
pages of my desire. of possibilities. of influence, and here he towered
above me seeming to gain height at will. his forearms bulged. the
path he took was a breathless sentence. he doubled back often his
finger at his lips in thought. he hinted at passion, tugged at my
sleeves, my cover. i held on to his voice like a scent, luxurious. i
adored him like my only audience. he spoke of marbled floors
peacock plumes perfumed baths graceful servants silver sapphires
chrome broadleaved trees year-round harvest a fat book contract
marvellous devices to do dishes or herd cattle instant ice cream
perfect rhubarb pie $600 per bushel of barley. rain. everything.
anything.

   i was gasping for breath.
   as if kicked.

   fell into step beside him. fell into his words.

i told him what i dreamed of while he quietly peeled a hard boiled egg held it between two manicured fingers. his teeth glinted extravagantly.

i found myself
famished.

seized.

friday, june 24

one evening he crouched down in the pasture precisely between the ground and the twilight sky. imprinting both. hunched just so. exactly centered so he wore the sky like a turban the soil like slippers. he held the grass the trees the moon the stars the cool air close taking these things the symbols the careless surfaces and held them close. intimate. handed them to me in his absent expressions of surprise. expectation

"These are my favourite lines. I'll whisper them. 'I have taught you that the sky in all its zones is mortal . . . Let me now re-emphasize the extreme looseness of the structure of all objects.' "
—Alice Gull

47

he told me the history of sleep. it was the spirit world
trickling into our nerve endings, leaking like a rainbow oil spill into
our stone senses. it was temptation, unleashed desire to a fervent
man who threw garbled curses at every night like a stray mongrel.
how many mistook it for death, like they did many other things, the
fantastic notions of death injuring life. he told me the fear of sleep
that i held. the way i prepare my bed, pray tensely, stare at the dark
as if it would make me disappear. how the dark inhabited sleep,
suspended the world, how no light spilled into my room, glinted off
my glasses propped on the bedside table or the dust on the mirror.
my sleep was absolute. all embracing. i discarded my dreams like
old paperbacks. garbled insanity, undiscovered colours, i thought.
they spilled off me come morning. set aside. but the devil said no.
no.

he knew rejection.

he told me he was king of my sleep. (he did not call himself
king, i think he balked at the word, struggled, toyed with a few
words: shepherd maybe, guardian, or architect, but i finished the
sentence for him in my eagerness for order.) all that bubbled in my
sleep, the wandering of mind, the world it arranged, the words that
half-formed my throat, the motion my eyes followed, hyper in my
deepest secrets, the precise spurts of adrenalin, the minute muscle
twitches and tremors, all fell into his hands. at night i was his
audience. the dark listened. this was the realm of the strange, the
unfathomable, the unreasonable, the unproductive. where we slept
or slept with him. he was the king of sleep. the sandman he
whispered. sleep is not.

i told him a dream and he said yes, yes, of course. it was
vaguely orange and slid against itself like two films overlapped.
there was fire against sunlight against starlight. afterimages when
you close your eyes and my hands were pools of green water. forests
grew from my lap. the devil said yes, sure, positively.

the sun settles like an old thought, the fade smooth, elegant.
he would argue for my salvation. he gestured his arms open, palms
turned outward speaking of possibilities, and out they spilled from
him. he asked me had i ever entertained the thought of him as my

lover. my throat stumbled, men loving men. he was sad, said it
could be magic. i said, yes, yes, it could.
i suppose.

      and he would fold the cover over me to keep me safe. his
words closed in me.

      near sleep, verging, i thought, roundabout, perhaps, i could.
      sleep is.

vagabond lines . they
. wander
from outside . he
invades dust
a pill . between
points . a hitch
. of destination
evading pails . he turns over
a graveside blur
stopping . here and .
upsetting routine
tumbling down . down
roads . opening backstreets
. leaving . gaps
an erratic memory . astray
. random plans
undoing his dirty pants relieving making himself
invisible. you see him leer at daughters you wish you had.
eat from garbage bins hands and face smeared pleased
undeniable. farts uncontrollable. you see him take hours.
cradle them. until he finds himself lost again.

vagabond blues (that street would take you to him –
opposite to intention instead – the dizzying one. fly.)

grin and then he says, "that tree with the low
branches is magic, you know."

you know what they say about him. he smells of. vague
words. labels
your thoughts.
turns himself out.
inside . your mind

wanders

you cannot remember him. few see him twice, you
see. without fluency. at night you may hear him sing in front
of the theatre or behind the cafe around the corner in a field
of ripe rye at your back door low and sad.
      pisses on steps with the sound of crisp rain.

      a small boy i know saw him. laughed fascinated.
frightened a little. guilty under our gaze he called to him.
      "hey, old man, you okay?"
      hazarding touch he helped him up when he fell. went
to him under cover of errands. gave him an apple. a bill. a
pop from the gas station where he worked. gave him
directions to the next town. pointed.

      the vagabond left. never came back

tuesday, june 29

what it comes down to is a question of scale. the devil and me.

we watched the sunset a few evenings ago. as the sun grew large and orange, celebrating its descent, swelling to land against the unforgiving horizon, the field fell into relief, the coop, the bluffs of willow, the fences, the scattered herd, the black and white holsteins struck ebony. became stark anticipations of night. detail leapt. drifted.

the sun opened its arms to the earth, spreading along its belly, a thin embrace.

a solitary cow stood at the juncture, the centre of the sun as it coasted half way. farewell. the cow eclipsed it with a brilliant dark casting a shadow miles to our feet. and then passed. the motion constant. terrifying.

scale came sudden. distance turned under the changing light, flooded into our eyes, the instant of surprise-breath. the location of the cow arched through the twilight. the sun, the horizon, the cow, our pastures, our neighbour's oats, our scramble to find a rope to lead the cow back. staples and a hammer to fix the fence. the devil asked if i knew what it was like to be chained to the sun.

a question of scale.

                    frozen hum
                              ming
          bird

                    its wings in mid

still   you look through

                              its inches its
                              black eyes black
                                        ice

          (green-blue stray there . . . or no)

                    sweet need lures you
                              the purple throats spits

its memory of blur
                              impossible if it did not exist

its feet so small
                    they cannot bear the weight

     of your gaze

          futhuffufhuffuthuthuhfuftufhuffuhhuhftuhfuhfuhhfuh

          fuhtufhuhfuhfutfutflutflit flit-t t   t   t

tsing

there is something
        in the way
   you moved

    the stray motion
            stringing motion by blur
something vague tucked into your pocket
                looped round your neck

    something in between
  you here   and then here

i've caught you there before

            (shy your red cheeks dirty
                what's more you peeked at your feet
                    a shiny apple fallen there)

    but this dapper and lean now
  i don't know this shutter skip
        this in-between scene
                        hardly recognize the guy

                    (he was a handsome devil
                    i had to hand it to him)

                    but i was left out
  between-times
        caught daydreaming

  my recollections
            my precious pictures of you
        evidently, all for nothing
    stranded while time slips into
                        a brand new you

mirror (mir'er) n. – a surface that reflects undiffused light to
    form an image of an object: something that gives a true
    representation of something else; v. – to reflect, repeat,
    imitate, resemble, adumbrate, mimic, simulate,
    conterfeit another.

            again you gasp at the
            gap between seeing your
                    self and yourself

            give yourself   up as lost

hop

     scotch to

  to it good

      & back again easy

  begin skip

     the crazy squares

  tilting slim

     you balanced

the edge oblivion

     scant order of chalk

  numbers curl by

     mark your feet

  concrete stutter

     picking up stone

  clutched words

     hop you back

  to a heaven

     teeter

the devil coiled in the grass sweet and wet beside the
sidewalk
he whispers vertigo
breezes by a distracted glance
prays for rain
slick
a suggestion perhaps
step this way my pretty

singing ice cream

a skinned knee stumble

thursday, july 2

    *i had only been there once as a kid. little Ellen was in an
accident. she had been stepped on by a Hereford bull and ruptured a
spleen. the Heron family lived on the edge of the foothills next to us.
their old black International wouldn't start in the cold and they
didn't have a phone so they had hitched up a quarterhorse to an old
sleigh. i spotted them going by the north section and dad and i went
after them. when we caught up with them El was unconscious,
slumped in the seat, her white face shiny with sweat. Mr. Heron
and dad lifted her into the truck next to me. our breath careful in
puffs until the cab warmed up. dad was talking but my mind could
not quite get around the slightness against me. a strand of her hair
stuck to my lip. near town i moved my arm around her waist
only to have her come to and elbow me away. she fought for
breath pushing at my chest. angry and hard against me. as if i
was the bull i guess. the hospital was a busyblur that smelled like
a bathroom. a nurse bundled El into another room and we went
home.*
    *a week later El and her dad came by to thank us. he was a
tall stilted man with a spiky beard and thin calloused hands. El
avoided my gaze at first but then began to look me up and down,
almost contemptuously and it made me blush. it was enough to
make us notice each other at the post office or the co-op or the cattle
drive. thoughts of El filtered through the tangle of my every dream.*
    *one day, a year or so later, mom called me with a twinkle in
her voice that instantly made me wary. you know the voice. ja-a-ay.
peered around a doorway to see El standing, her hands on her hips,
an impatient crease on her forehead. she pulled me out the door and
i found myself following her down a grown-over cutline with her
ringing voice filling me up. the sky was bluer than it should have
been. birds were everywhere.*
    *soon we came to a place, more of a place than i had ever
been before. El and i stood at a point where the forest fell into the
sky. we teetered there, over a bowl of woods ringed with towering
blocks of grey stone. my feet surged when they stepped from the
leaves onto rock. El laughed, told me that these were the rimrocks.*

she led me down through a crevice, the cold rock and lichen rubbing our shoulders, the sky a river above us. in the stand of forest below the wind stopped. stopped so completely we became aware of our own breathing. our voices seemed foreign there. our laughter seemed small in that space but grew larger booming off cedar and granite. she touched my hand once then looked at the sun to check the time. i asked if i could see her again and she said, probably not.

since then, i've heard talk of her fighting with her family. from what people say recently, it seems she wanted her father to give her some land to live on. she has three brothers and her father apparently thought she should be married at her age. it was quite a ruckus. most people thought she was a little crazy. i don't know how it turned out.

an excommunication suite
courting retribution

all the time i was telling you love
not speaking the air
that split my tongue

isn't the spell alone
        worth that
suspension a tempest
        a swirling
        abandon sweet sweet on the tongue

the toll of vespers
        bright against your impatience

the messages rolled
under the chortle of carrier pigeon
creeping behind sentries
climbing your trellis   your lovely trellis
a late ring of voice
        sound corded with distance
the lines tapped
        trapped in red velvet lines

touch forbidden
i chose & i chose
longing

with want
        trapped heavy
                in vestments
i fled
flew into
        you, winged still
        flutters in your ear

the time between replies like exile
                    unruly
the air cutting my tongue

expectant
i send &

i send once more

friday, july 13

    now maybe i'll tell you – that first morning we met, the very first thing i noticed about him, it wasn't his skin or his voice or his posture – my eyes instantly realized a huge difference between the devil and most mortals. i didn't make a big issue about it at the time and casually averted my eyes as is proper but, boy, it sure made an impression. i'm not saying it's a hang-up or anything and i realize that all of us are endowed in different ways but, man o man, this was something. it borders on the absurd, the larger-than-life, the fantastic, the earth-shattering, a massive leap from real-life, a legend in the making.

    the first thing i noticed on that crazy morning was – the guy had no prick! nothing.

    just like captain america or spiderman – just a flat space – empty.

    how could i not notice.

(detail: Frances Goya, *Saturn Devouring One of His Children*, 1823)

a hunger stilling time
melting legs   mesmerized
by the wind he is flying

the forest on his back
        the ground lurches
beneath his wild run
the rage and bellow
        cracking birch bows
lakes sucked into his lungs

you hear him coming
            know him well

the moon may hide you

the taste of fear
        teeth bared
glaring like guilt from the indistinct
        leaping between your fears
    your own urge to devour
            eating at you
                licking your wounds

slipping to madness
        a lip curl and snarl
    you feel him close
        on either side of here
            surrounding now
    almost inside
        eyes wild
        he is looking at you
        he is looking at you

– what is your favourite letter in the alphabet, devil?

– mmmmmmmmm, i think the letter l, the end of evil
and the beginning of love. or maybe s, just because you can
go sssssssssssssssssssssssssssssss with an s and you can make
one into ones. but if you are thinking of what to call me,
think about the letter h. l, though, yes l. El walks up the third
cutline off the east quarter up to the rimrocks every evening
just before dusk. Ask me more.

– oh. what is your favourite word?

– oh . . . or maybe j. or maybe murmur because it
slows time like making love in the afternoon. or maybe or. or
maybe maybe. or maybe favourite.

– every evening?

– an h is empty, the sound of air, a release, yes, a
release.

. . . departures are everything, are they not . . .

I have decided to give Catch my collection. Over tea I hand
her the thick floppy book, my lips are tight, uncertain.
This, then, becomes my part, my half of the conversation.
I reach it towards her in lieu of my name. The scrapbook is
heavy in her hands. Loaded. She runs her fingers over the
edge of a photograph, the gloss, the white creases, the
browned newsprint. The handwriting splays and peters
out in places. Glue splotches come off in clear flakes
smelling sharp and high. Some pages are ripped, parts
missing or thrown in. Loose. The spine is splitting. She
reads it and on each page displays something to me,
sometimes surprise, sometimes fear, her eyes hiding,
sometimes comfort. When she looks up, there is
something more, something just between me and her.
She tells me what she sees, there, in my scrapbook. Her
breath smells like cucumber. I begin to think about
departures.

friday, july 26

he craves extremes, like his nerves were a novelty. he
wanted to see the snake pits after he read that piece in The Tattler.
he invited El and Apology without me knowing and by 10:30 this
morning i found myself careening down aimless gravel roads in
El's International. our eyes peered into scrub and rocky meadows
looking for the pits. the heat burgeoned. the radiator hissed and we
listened, our backs wet on the hot vinyl. El was in my lap and i
didn't know why we were out here, his whims controlling our lives.
we were wrapped in his hands like a hot steering wheel. El smelled
like cows' breath and sage. a strand of her hair stuck to my lip. i let
it.

                interlake garter snakes
                    & snakes
                    & snakes like hair
                the devil called rapunzel
                        took them to the pits

            there   somewhere between poems
                he stopped singing
                        fell from the car

            the ground swayed
                    whispering medusa loose

        he animated their fascination
        the force that cranes necks   goosepimpled
                nerves to the writing   lost in the roll
    and twining of bodies   revulsion and fear imprints
        left behind   motion in sand   shift and twist
    three spasmed against   their feet in passion   passion
a fugue in skin   extremes of touch   tightrope
    they longed to roll too   let their hair   down   knot

        have you entertained the thought
        love, a braid wrapping and unwrapping
        anticipation

        and then we went under

                    "They say snakes go blind for a
                    while before they shed skin for
                    the last time."
                    —Toni Morrison

                        67

our dissent didn't unfold as planned
didn't seem inevitable at all

the dark surged, the crevice caught, hooked into our
desires (have you ever entertained the thought)
the cave entrance, a lover's lips moist and clean the
smell of used breath, memory scent, sweet but
musty filled with the imagined; further knots of
serpents, lost worlds of the pale eyeless, remains of a
struggle, a hermit's rags and baubles, a bandit's hoard and
last frenzied need, a fugitive's last meal scattered and rotting,
perhaps flame, a river to take you away endlessly entwining
you to roots, a dead body, its skeletal grin and tales of the
neverending, the void, the ever after
the closet of dirt and clay we hung our fears in the
dark, grabbed our stories, stuffed them into corners and
holes, refused our sunlight eyes

scratches on the wall, the worm's work

a cool breeze jostled hell from our lips a lie

no, no, we would go down, it was okay

underneath rocks hum a consistency hone away settled seeds
the hard cup rolling time so sightless knolls and slopes the
angles set to challenge sump energy the limp unnoticeable
stone under tons of air chant a morning thrum through binge
easy veins and bumps of fossil the thoughts ringing encased
in warm consideration the shift cozy into stiff back the chairs
of ocean slopping on granite eyelids you thumb pick at lazy
wounds rain hands of islands sigh over your skin scent out
the huddled exhalations of your domain unnerved limestone
patches bleed out clamoring quartz and mica squint tiny bits
scattered but deep in contemplative lotion sleep the molten
creases patience quickens churning pallor ocher motion slow
unmalevolent stroke of ceaseless broad sweep of sanctuary
spoon no throaty voice cajoles the tampered lip the cracked
lid just barely ajar the alien sweat in mirrors cringe at pointed
eyes underground murmur sound testing the pesky heavens
the pull of nagging sun an untapped temper resounding with
slow

the ground gave way often the walls crumbling to the touch.

the devil lit a torch startling.

the cavern flew into

relief.

stratified like memory.

our watching

a digging

the limestone eyelid. grit under the fingernails

of our mind

vision flapped shadows against

corners and hollows.

sounds clung

then leapt at odd angles careened

into forever or thumped

into your clothes and hair.

memory slapping them

away.

stalactites of fear.

of love.

the devil showed the way

broke trail

began.

surrounded down.

again.   he was weeping when we

weren't looking.

again. i think i cried too

contemporary fear
　　your body catch
skin quiver lip
　　　　curl and dart

at an absence
　　the eye grasp at dark
shudder at lack of upward
　　　the round arc a word
　you wish a lullaby
　　　　　of sky

that scream you dream
　　when their ears appear
　closed and farther away
　　　　than you can carry
　　throwing your throat anyway

　your body actual
bending to a displacement

the devil he
　fills up
　　　　　caves you into his arms
　　dispels you familiar
　　　　smells endless

occupies your time
wraps himself around
the panic of new colours
none primary at least
a name you can see
until you return
a quick pack of reason
to spark your cupped hands
the flare dribbling
hot onto your palm

love be damned

Appearances: Photo #5
the old man his clothes earth-coloured cracked and torn he greets you like he always has clear eyes his mouth entrancing already moving in story as you approach arms spread wide hands out beckoning.

and there, that day, the four of them, Jay, El, Apology, and the devil, found a place so free of light, so absent of glint or glow, that when they closed their eyes the glare of afterimages from the surface was blinding

their breathing made an undulating rush, their heartbeats a troupe of percussionists, blood roared, bellies gurgled, throats croaked and thrummed of their own accord, feet thundered, scraped, eyelids clicked

sparks jumped from the smallest touch, finger against finger, hand on waist, chin on chest, lip against lip

blue-white, grey-green, violet, magenta, that startling red flicked at the dark, fringing motion, tracking the intimate brushes against skins

the devil rubbed his own shoulders and silvery wings flashed outward, Apology ruffled her hair and flames shot up from her scalp, Jay's hand occasionally touched El's as they stood afraid, shoulder to shoulder, sparks leapt back and forth, even just before contact, jumping across, anticipating, charting thumb to palm, finger to wrist, thigh against thigh, and there was glow, the taste electric on your tongue

psssssssst, a secret is something you tell someone else

and there was this place, more of a place than ever before, a cavern warm with breath, the walls soft with sand and a river rushing through the sound huge carrying your balance away reduced to bare touch, the liquid everything wrapped in arms in dark, the heat tugged at clothes and beautiful skin slid through the dark and wet, their nakedness a tribute to the deep

mediums mixed, the damp air, the easy river, the fine sand, the slick skin melted in and out, the press of a tongue, there, suspended, held, coaxed, higher and higher, until voices began pleading naming each other naming a fingertip reach of ecstasy, speaking release, telling the other to let go, just let go, desperate for fire

and then, of course, there was light teased from the dark the flicker from the devil's finger a star wince in his palm, a burst of white, orgasm swooped from the shadows flew toward the roof, a singe, a slight burn, and settling to rest

i think i saw god, someone whispered

the devil lit a pile of sticks by the river, they sat close around the fire watching the way it swayed, made eyes infinite and sheltered, surprised at the lines and bulges that their fingers and hands had known, they watched the fire, its waver, its leap of faith into the open air

months later, there would be a catch to this occasion, a catch that not even the devil could conceive of

in the light everyone became aware of the scars on Jay's belly. red swirling flesh twisted into a vortex on his torso. skin reformed into a dizzying pattern. he turned against the light, cradled his arms in front of him but the silence brushed at the knowledge, the question stuttering voices. he sat a ways from the fire. began.

chore time – i was late, lagging – alone, and it was
okay – the house & me – it came from the chimney and attic i
guess – i-i-i heard my dad talk about a chimney f-fire before –
angry – furious – fire was everywhere – it growled, wounded
it went crashing through me – smacking the kitchen table,
my boots melted to the floor – i s-s-slowed the rhythm of the
flames – i slowed and slowed – almost stopped i almost did –
lifted she lifted me – i-i-i-i . . . the words choked, sputtered,
rested in the arms of El. his skin hot to the touch.

monday, july 27

i remember the time, not long after he showed up, the devil and i were the last ones out of the outhouse pit. we had all fallen in and were up to our armpits in shit. could barely breathe. we lifted the smaller ones out first, the kids still howling at our misfortune. then it was just me and the devil. he locked his hands together and said, 'up.' i offered the same, we looked at each other for a long time there, bowed. he said, and i just remembered this, it didn't really sink in at the time, he said, 'look at me and look through me, preacher man, look through me' and then told me, 'climb' and closed his hands together again. i stepped up, on his hands then shoulders, even the top of his head before i was out. boost, that is the word i am looking for. he gave me a boost up. it was then that i stopped being afraid of the devil. told him thanks with a voice hoarse from too long without use. when we had him out, he pronounced that if cleanliness was close to godliness then well . . . redemption was a long long way away.

"A literary work is a communal act."
—Michael Ondaatje

Jay's farm is still snug against that range of hills I hear called the Knot. If you were to come from the west where the rutted highway lets go of those maddening woods, past the quiet tree eyes, past the insane loggers alongside the road lugging their gear (watching, always watching you go by), if you were to come from that direction, the farm unfurls, flaps below you like a six-fingered hand, and it sees you are going to fall off the edge into its palm. But nobody ever would come that way, except if they suddenly had found their way out of the bush after years and years of. . . . But nobody ever would. When I first came from the east, the long fields folded away from me so that the far edges were lost in a morning mist or sunset or something, I can't remember what. This may be the last time I see it. The highway is paved now so I can sit on the shoulder without worrying about idiots flying by and nicking my paint job even more with that loose gravel. Tired of all this. If nothing turns up soon I'm heading back. Fuck the devil. He ain't here. It's -45 C for christ's sake. The woman on the radio didn't seem too flustered by that kind of cold, just went on about preserves and rutabagas or something. I can't handle it though. I panicked when my fingers nearly froze to the car handle and my upholstery cracked when I sat down. When I look up at the clear sky I can see little arcs around the sun, like it's all wrapped up tight and small so we can all freeze in hell down here. Well whatever, I'm throwing in the towel soon.

There goes Jay now, punctual as always. Back and forth he goes between those little buildings carrying stuff and buckets and doing god-knows-what. And those fashionable coveralls, he's a gem that's for sure. I wish it was him I was trying to catch. It would be too easy. I could just smell him out with all that cowshit he wades through. I could just dress up as a cow and dangle a tit. Ha. Stupid hick could just spill. I know he'd hiding something. But I'm tired, sick and tired of this hole. It's too cold for the devil.

There he goes up to break the ice on the dugout. Every morning he stand there and chips away with a crowbar. Chip chip chip chip chip. It takes forever. Always he does this. He just doesn't get it. Chip chip chip chip. He must be dumb as a stone. And to think he might have had the devil on his hands. To think. I wish I could have seen that. Ha.

sideshow is
when i yelled encore or something like that in the dead of 4:00
or thereabouts
and am not quite
        aware why

sometimes sometimes he
        would appear
    his face

        half   white half black
        exactly
                              a silhouette insinuation

and then he would repeat my slightest move
every motion   alto again
words an echo   a perfect cadence
                            a sound
                            mirrorrim
                            sound a

        reverb
        inging

        & when he laughed   or cried
        his make-up masks & show
            pressing horizons upon horizons across
        his expression   a fugue in D minor with exquisite highs
                    his eyes the echo of applause

the line between cracked/creased
                            blur red
                    the line   gone

    the exit precise now

The love affair between Jay and El grew like a comfortable habit after the caves. They met every evening after milking up by the Rimrocks. They watched each other make their way across the last pasture, noticed new things about the way each walked, moved through trees, climbed fences, the way each watched the other watching. They touched hands when they met, remembering the sparks. They spoke low, about the herds, which cows were due to calf, how the barley looked, and, even lower, something about the weather I couldn't catch. They laughed when they talked about the devil and Apology, recalling their latest antics.

At the rocks their talk became smaller, bits of wonder, pointed words lifted away by the winds. Their backs side by side, a gentle symmetry with the rocks, the arch of hills, the horizon breaking into a grin.

One evening, they brought hammers, yanked out staples and rolled up a long portion of barbed-wire fence. Jay kissed a scrape on El's wrist. I tasted salt, groped my way through the poplar saplings to the road.

their eyes squinched up to the sun
tongues on lemon

the dark seeming sweet

friday, august 13

    *one morning just before chores, three men in a bright
orange truck crept down the east gravel road as if afraid of waking
something up. the devil lingered by the pump-house to watch. the
truck stopped every few hundred feet and an arm or two would fold
out of a window cocked in definite directions. repeatedly. finally the
men tumbled out sending plumes of dust into the air when they
flapped and thumped their thighs. they pulled a bulky engine off the
back of the truck that had a tall auger attached. on rusted metal
wheels it rolled off the back on planks and down into the ditch by
the barbed wire fence. 'doin' some seismic work' one said as if to
apologize for the racket, or the time of day, or his moustache.*

    *the devil watched wide-eyed. soon the charge had been set
and there was a spectacular suspended silence before the rumbling
report crawled up everyone's spines. from the cab of the truck a
print-out emerged with feathery hills and valleys, the layers and
knots of soil and rock shouting up a landscape of ink and white. the
foreman grunted and they got set to move on.*

    *the devil began fussing and gesturing wildly, 'wait . . . wait
and take a reading of this.' he reached into the cab, flipped a few
random switches. running hard he leapt over the barbed wire fence
into the field. there, he stood silhouetted on a slight rise, his arms
above his head in a pinnacle, toes pointed outward, his bony frame
arched and rigid, beautifully balanced. for the longest moment he
stood that way, perfectly still, poised, frozen, his skin gleaming like
red stone. his form etched, sculpted from the dirt, the air. then, he
shattered. a hollow stunned pop followed by a roaring release of air
and sound rushed outward. the men only had time to flinch as
shards shot against their skin. they yelped and hopped around their
hands on their bellies and necks and shoulders. blinking and
cursing they found only a pink liquid trace where the glass had hit,
the skin left unbroken. the ground still shook, dust rose from the
summerfallow, birds started in the poplars, leaves popped loose, a
wind began from right here. the men shifted their weight, spread
their feet to maintain their balance. voices wove in and out of the
roar. wailing, laughing, howling voices, voices that screamed,
shouted into the open, they belched, farted into the spinning wind,*

those frightened voices that seemed to come from everywhere, wind devils played and dissolved on the road as the vibrations slowed and stopped. the men scrambled for the truck, faces pale. as they drove away they took furtive looks at the spurts of ink that had chugged out of the seismograph. one finally began reading . . .

---

the scrapbook's cover is curling in on itself. She gives it back careful not to let stuff fall out. Intent I reach to take it back. All of it. Perhaps too soon. Perhaps she needed more time to wander through its rough surfaces. Perhaps she wishes to keep it. She seems to hesitate. Then begins to pass it. Begins. Over.

Something falls out.

---

touch

against   the
  against   the
    against   the
      against   the
        against   the
          against   the
            against   the
              againstthe
              ainstth
              intth
              nstt
              stt
              tt
               t

                    ch

cabbage   [BRASSICA OLERACES] - Europe 500 B.C.

carrot   [RAUCUS CAROTE] - Afghanistan 500 B.C.

corn   [ZEA MAYS] - Central America 2000 B.C.

onion   [ALLIUM CEPA] - West Asia 4000 B.C.

rhubarb   [RHEUM RHAPONTICUM] - Asia Minor 3000 B.C.

       from the almanac of love – the traces of seasons and succulents. call me Mephistopheles and i will frown, call you pompous, refuse to meet you by the peas at dusk. call me, call me serendipity. call me hhhhhhhey. call me soon and i will pluck beans husk corn (the fine hairs brushing at your wrists) pick blueberries and pop them in your mouth sashay away – say shush.

wednesday, august 15

*had a dream – held it for a few days until it came distinct,
made a shape.*

*huge machines raked across the valley like a proper noun –
they drove into the ground, not turning soil like a plow or breaking
sod like a disc, but gouging with grey-green blades.*

they were looking for the devil.

*i was with him in a cave near the river. fire was everywhere
and the devil darted against the panicking walls like a bird in the
greenhouse. as i watched he changed shape. and again. over and
over as if searching for a face to escape by. strange pelts, scales,
grotesque limbs, gaping mouths flashed in front of me. the
machines rumbled overhead.*

*he came to rest finally in the shifting sand heaped near the
entrance to the cave. next to me he huddled trying to burrow
between me and the rock. the machines drew nearer. closing in.*

the ground leaked and inky blue. covered us all.

you may find

him kneeling in

the womb of your

sleep waiting

for red

emption

"Faith - n. Belief, without
evidence, in what is told by one
who speaks without
knowledge, of things without
parallel."
—Ambrose Bierce, *The Devil's
Dictionary*

maybe	may be
maybe	certain
maybe	when you're not looking magic things leap from cupboards the clouds, doubt, the pit of your stomach
	the lapse in conversation
	between me and you
maybe	my sons and daughters will appear in stories – sure of themselves in a neat expensive hard-cover world
maybe	a demon will reform rent a couch in a pipe-scented office and firmly establish an efficient business advising miscreants
maybe	the devil has a tuning fork that changes with mood swings and the tide
maybe	in grade seven when i was thrown out of class and sent to confess maybe i meant it what i said to him, maybe i meant it
maybe	the devil pleaded guilty unwillingly too soon maybe the devil was slandered maybe the devil doesn't control the media, doesn't get along with reporters and irritates anchormen, maybe the devil has hoofed feet because the devil is a scapegoat, a martyr, maybe the devil got caught playing dirty, laid his hand down too soon, had tumultuous sex out of wedlock, got caught giving god a blow job (a good one at that – lucky the hummer wasn't loaded), maybe he got caught red handed, maybe the devil lost an election, got appointed to the senate after a conflict of interest scandal but is living comfortably in Burnaby with a jaguar and a collection of Tom Thomson originals, maybe the devil was framed, maybe the devil has a delightfully rare disease, maybe catchy, maybe

the devil is ugly like the elephant man,
deformed with warts, horns, abscesses, extra
digits (just don't count him out), a third eye,
huge hooked incisors that gleam with love, a
hunchback and a large cumbersome bell,
inflamed skin, vestiges of an ancestral tail (a fine
tale-spinner), spock ears, beaming red irises,
scales, soft fur along his spine that you could
never mistake for hackles without raising a fuss
so soft you cannot resist touch, an acrobatic
tongue clicking to a spring-board tune, crazy
knees that pop deep in the night and you don't
care you just don't care

maybe   the bee knows exactly the threat of frost the
crystal possibilities inside

maybe   you are not loving me good

Appearances: Photo #1
    pale red a torn loincloth sagging chin belly eyes
ruffled in his humble tenacity another face with nothing left
to lose except perhaps a chance at death – a new kind of awe
– the bravery of staying otherwise

Apology and El and
sister the moon they
wound their arms round
wicked the flare of candles set
the cast iron sky aside
and skin they sang flesh
at the night sang satin
a net to spell lull
velvet lips knit seams
where to hide words flipping
memory like a veil
naked and hidden El's hand
Apology's belly a question
yes yes of course and i will
be there to catch
and dispel

laugh making
                                    me

    she tickled me in

        the ribs

                            sent me

fleeing

                doubled
                me

                up

tuesday, august 27

one morning as the night faded back, cornered against the horizon, i despaired at ever getting a good crop. last year a spring drought hardened seeds, shrivelled sprouts, stunted all the crops. only the wheat came through the dry okay. the year before the rain was ceaseless, never stopped, day after day until the crops were flooded out. only the oats came through alright. this year everything looks good but now i have to try and fit the swathing into the weather. look at the sky. should i cut or not? if i do and the swathes don't dry enough before it rains again, the grain rots on the ground. if i wait too long the grain over-ripens and the stalks buckle and the crop lies down so i can't cut. so what do i do? devil, what do i do? my frustration clouded my eyes, made my head droop.

i'd do anything if i could just tell the weather.

anything.

"The trouble with argument is that it moves the whole struggle onto the Enemy's own ground . . . Do remember you are there to fuddle him. From the way some of you young fiends talk, anyone would suppose it was our job to teach."
—Screwtape

anything or the devil take you

anything you would have me sing, releasing the sound,
letting it fall where it may, wherever it may, and, it just may
in may

anything i can do yes anything

anything you would have me sing for rain have me look into
a crystal ball brew a fine dance for you i would do anything
anything love

anything i could make you rain from nothing the drops a
torrent from your unknowing eyes salt stinging the power to
do it but no

anything to know the swoop of the cumulus the settle of arid
the jet stream bulge winding away your hopes the
stratosphere signs you would do anything to be uncontrolled
by the dance of warm and cool anything for me

anything that thing which i most desire anything i wish a
return return to me you could turn me in you could take me
in take me take me

anything is infinite, callous

anything i want would be a single something from you,
intimate and kind

anything i will

anything i will give you: this: at dawn go to the Gap Marsh
near the delta, look for a healthy bladderwort, frail thin
looking plants that grow alone and identifiable by their deep

green colour and their tendriled pouches that are shaded purple and catch insects. it is important you find a plant that is standing in less than half a centimetre of water, no more. pull up the plant whole, it will come up easily. beneath the base of its stalk will be a stout tuber-like root. it will be pale white and ribbed. split it off from the stalk. this next bit you must do soon. take the root, dry it off, and cut it as precisely in half as possible. take one half and hold it above your palm with the fresh cut facing down. now if a drop of moisture falls that means that at least ten days of dry weather is coming. if no moisture issues then rain is coming soon. if the drop is tinged red then drought is imminent. replace the root for it will produce a new plant.

anything is beyond me, but here now, love, let me come with you

wet

the earth breathes

earth into my mouth

touch yourself think of me without breathpause

monday, august 19

The devil and I went to town.

He was insatiable. The flashing light, the shadows, they drew us inside.

The first night he pulled us into a pool hall called LOS ANGELES AMUSEMENTS, although someone had spraypainted a T after LOS. Down down flights of cracked cement stairs. We got a table fast considering the line-up. The guy behind the counter stuttered, wide-eyed.

— what g-game, g-guys?

The devil leapt to my side, whispered.

— Them all.

The devil's eyes were already rubbing against the plush banks, the warm wood frames, the cool balls racked against green, row upon row.
I assumed my teacher voice, spoke of breaks, hooks, bank shots, spins, order, shape, etiquette, form, the graces. The devil took up two balls, the cue ball and the eight.

— Why is this one white, and this one black?
— Well, I . . . I don't . . . I-i-i-it's not . .
— Let's try this.

With a wink the pockets disappeared and only three balls remained on the table, the cue ball and two red. We played billiards. No balls fell, no hard clacks, no balls slammed into the backs of pockets. No easy progression, cue-eight-pocket. Just the roll, rub, play of possibility. Glances and grazes. The banks true and lively. A crowd gathered to watch. The motion elegant and gentle. Touch all.

The second night we went to this bar. It was busy, dark, warm with bodies. We drank strange liquids – the devil knew the bartender. Beer, boomers, prairie fires, screwdrivers, paralyzers, zombies, gin martinis ('dust off the olive,' the devil said), beer, rye and coke, scotch and water. Our tongues rolled over them all. And the devil danced. His hair was perfect. He spun and sprawled over the dance floor, his hips rubbing against a galloping crowd. The gulping faces breeze-blown. Drinking him up. And those hips. Hips and flying feet. Fleet beneath his twist. The bar spun and I was singing off key. Street lights appeared against the sudden bricks of the walls. A stage grew and a poet began reading. He shouted and made rude noises. He leaned close and painted himself. Red. Let's try this, he sang.

"Really, it were enough to
fright the Devil himself to meet
himself in the dark."
—Daniel Dafoe

picked up the instrument played just
                    and then
        when he plays   he plays on
                        slow and smooth
            the groove   the let
                    breath and lay back
        slump in notes and   bright the blues
                    soothe the slick line
            low lifting low   you slide
                        down the slow motion
        the sounds sip at your
                    attention he snaps
                you up sends you under
            currents of bends   and hook
        the sound of sibilants up close
                    he took you
                by surprise on by they swing
                by the way he played   deadly wise
                    he played the notes
            time slimmed   and weightless
                white zoning on brighter white
                    and hours he played
            your motions slip
                        the dip of knees
                    twist of hips
            anticipates his trill and moan
        steepstraw notes   closing on you
                        stolen notes
            bandit clips and scamper through
                    splashed a riff
                fingers gone stiff with planting
                resting in a roll of lull
            waiting for liquid
                        he declined
        he played you
                    for a fool
        he played

                        slow

sunday, august 29

  leaping from a dream, i sprinted to the bathroom, noticed,
for what must be the first time, the colour of my skin. my arms in
the terse linoleum light, the shades of brown tan, the pink palm,
fingertips, the shy blue veins. (the mirror rattled with my colours.)
my eyes, those looking at me, shifted up. (there was, as always, it
seems, a pause before recognition.) i studied the frail wisps like tree
bark of blue in my irises, the bulge of tear-ducts, the creases on my
lids, as if i had been folded too many times. crows feet clutching. i
watched the drop and catch of my lips as i mouthed my body, my
tongue surprise, bumpy and sluggish. (the mirror misting over
with my breath.) i watched my tongue search over my teeth, saw
the touch that said incisor and huge. followed the swirls and arcs of
hair as they swept down my chest, past the uneven pink stubs of
nipple. leaning in, i watched the fine lines sweeping across my skin,
bold on my palms, sheer on my forearms, belly, the head of my cock,
bundles of knee. (the mirror ducked and bent.) my bumpy feet
blue-grey with blood, the hard cup of my heel, the small bit of dirt
in the corner of my big toenail. fingers over the chapped patch of
skin on the inside of my thighs where they rub together. i wrapped
my hand around my calf, felt the muscle bunch up and slide as i
flexed. pulled at the tendon at the back of my knee wondering at
how distant it felt. like testing a fan belt or halter. i puffed out the
tuft of my pubic hair, flipped the ancient-looking bag, two large
Lima beans they seemed, a flimsy pod. i lifted my arms, watched the
sheaves of muscle settle, the air cheering in my armpit hair, and my
scent, i breathed in my own. i pitched my hand across my scalp, the
hollows and ridges, the flap of ear. watched my finger tip the fine
hairs at the back of my neck, the vibrating rush of my throat, the
lumpy gulp and gurgle. i penciled my thumb over the soft fur in
my bum crack, played the scale of my spine. all night i touched and
smelled and watched. my skin strange. a twitch beneath my finger.
my tongue speaking to my eyes. (i could, yes perhaps, i could.) my

body a script, a loose page. turn. a turn of phrase, a conversation
with myself, there in the bathroom glare. we spoke (yes, perhaps)
and you. (could, yes perhaps.)

"Time is measured not by
numerals on a clock face but by
the incidence of our
apprehended possibilities."
—John Berger

curled into. hunched back. the streets they. we descended to. shotgun. the devil riding. main street hissed with. from bars side doors. street noon sleep. drawn. the devil throwing up. the crowd they picked up. arms. pink on the street. bright. leaflets they blew into. in hands. rage. bits of discussion. an argument went. pushed to. dirty. from pink words. flapping down main. numbers. the sidewalk spilling. cracked. boom traffic clutter. horns. a rear view. mirror knocked. angry out window tire lurch. words thrown. up truck. on boulevard. blares. the sun repeating. spin the devil. and arrow south. whisper city. oh no. city we. are here. a billboard falls. flat face down. struck the. ground air carrying. dust in protest. shoes on asphalt against. clomp. the surfaces are. there. we become. more. wall street shy. the devil pointed south. sweat on. skin colours glistening. bunches. hesitations swept up. the crowd in. close. trespassing those. who. against. traffic left. a stalled car platform. leaping. the devil calling up. hey he said. hey. aimless was. specific. watch the faces they. grow. creased in. hunched. lip curl. the city awaits. use.

Appearances: Photo #3

the troll long lanky maniac eyes teeth spitting spider motions through swamp an animated hunger bushed the moon pushes full into the top right the landscape shivers and slides over

monday, may 3

    dark red fading to pink finger-tips palms. in each hand an egg pilfered warm. unruffled he met my accusing gaze. speckled with a question.

    my eyes fell onto his distended belly, the yoke on his neck

    i handed an apple to a third arm extending from his gaze.

    said
    (and we had words)

    sorry.

a torch was lit. carried by a stocky woman with graying hair and sandals. it was joined by more. that first torch lit another and further. lighting. ignition. windows, the glare in the. a boy warmed his hands, palms out. that first torch flashed through a broken grocery store window, thumped into a stack of boxes. spark catch. the fire spread quickly along neat aisles of big name brands, through breakfast cereals with pops and crackles, roared through the toilet paper and tampons going up in yellow bursts, bread, magazines gave off strange flames, blue-green and purple, potato chips in plumes of smoke, dog food with a puff of stink, sizzling produce. the flower shop in a sweet-smelling rush. the store erupted howling and snapping. the heat built up, buckled girders and support beams, beginning with a solitary explosion and then a barrage, cans and bottles began to burst open. resounding blasts fragments of flaming metal and glass shot out streaking the night like fireworks. whole cans humming over our heads to land on the pavement still spinning. containers buzzed and whirred into the cool food splattering over the street. wondrous smells for miles. finally the roof gave way and plummeted to the ground shuddering the ground. safeway. the sign in the front tumbled free face down in the turning lane, sparking.

gone to press

a limp justification of a front cover
a defining font
florid bindings
(if i could only copy right)
rolled pressing skin
chlorophyll free & recyclable
unaided and floating in design
    a thing responded
saddle stitched and bucking spontaneous combination
slap of carbon
intrusion in ink

collated haphazard
flash script/return
there is no
thin thing unturned
(the epitaph, you jest)

yeah and here i am bickering with fathers

jesus crowns insurgences
& texts wading through shelves
words fly they do
up
the climax
here i
am uncertainty   )

obtaining a certain circulation
on consignment, of couse but far
out of edit
oriole control
the last line
        spasms

"A marvelous read . . . could not put this book down for love nor money . . . achievement of the year"

"A must for any avid reader . . ."

"When I read this book I thought of you . . . good grammar throughout . . ."

in the printshop of night
you collate my dreams

the oversized templates flooded with light
                    & dark
        the camera-ready original
            touched up a bit

after you use blue ink
        the invisible kind
    to bracket my thought
sign your name

the cutter shored up edges
your book flew into my hands
perfectly bound
the paper was moss-oriental flecked
                    twenty-pound test
the font helvetica bold
    with roman italics
the ink royal lavender
        scrolling against my fingers
my cover was blown
            up photographs of violence
the motions blurred
        faces contorted
sometimes you re-arranged
    the pages, left some out
            added bits from other jobs

i checked
sometimes you would tip that valve
        the ink faded to white space with faint impressions
you could feel on your eyelid

i worried about you there your words
    vulnerable flesh in that landscape
        the blades and gears
you curled there at night
  the maniac machines asleep still warm
the dry smell of paper like wheat
    sharp ink like diesel
i imagine
black splattered   paper cuts stung
your skin pressed to paper
    the typeface smudged with fear-sweat

i imagine you thought of me

(detail: John Berger, *G.A. Novel*, 1972)

> madness
>   you name me
> numerous
>   call me profuse
rampant

>   do not fear a crowd

i press on all sides jostle
>   scents of food body fluids
>   perfume stark edge
of cloth
>   cling to
> the heat off
>   bodies washing close
>   °

you may wander through me
>   taste the murmur of my voice
>   hear my discontent

>   my disruption

i am a march a barricade
>   a riot of words
>   if you come to
>   skirt the furtive streets
>   seize a weapon
>   stick knife scythe
>   pitchfork

if you come along
>   join with someone who speaks
>   a language you may or may not understand
>   who will give you wheat bread
>   potato wine, rice, an apple

the words singing in your stomach
you may be afraid
                    not try to pronounce my names
                              watch the news of my death
                                        the next morning
            but still
                    the crowd moves self-less

        the city waits for use

and then there was fire. fire from nowhere it seemed to come from the concrete from the glass building without fuel. it licked up the side of the Billington Complex. its glow could be seen in a few windows of the First National. down Success Avenue more started adding light to the host of torches. streetlights were paled. the night became hot. shadows swayed, bent into angles. shadow undulated into light, light into shadow. the crowd pressed into its dance.

the police had wedged into the intersection and now stood shields held close to reflect the glare. a milling uneasy blue. voices echoed over the scene. and officer spoke of order. spoke of commandments. spoke of trespassing and of property rights. someone laughed. there will be no miracles here.

a bearded man split away, skirted the barricade of cars. he walked toward the leveled rifles tearing open his shirt to bare his chest. screamed so that spit scattered from his mouth. he screamed shoot. shoot me. his chest bared. shoot.

grievance wore thin that night. for hardship, a trigger pulled quicker, collection, a cold imbalance. these appeared on the streets this night twisting suspended. speaking. the message hung.

the streets were astounded. called him insinuation.

and the devil appeared again this time his simmering skin shone out from between the huge green letters I and N. someone pointed. voices hollered, whistled, more faces looked up. up on the thirty-first floor, propped in the middle of the green landmark DOMINION sign. the fifteen foot letters made him look sharp and dramatic. fires panicked out of windows now catching paper, melting plastic, crumpling desks, disintegrated software, peppering carpet, bursting through doors. unchecked.

the devil spoke.

he spoke in a voice that singed and sang through the fires, through the angry tussle of voices, through the sweat between fist and police revolver. faces turned. eyes focused through the smoke on him. orange light glinted off his eyes, his bare chest, the palms of his hands as he opened them to the crowd. the crowd took him in. his words were engulfed, swallowed. frantic megaphone threats failed to overpower him, his voice trailing through the crowd from all directions, a murmur. perhaps even a leap of faith.

Apology strolled below. the streets received her feet for the first time. they were as surprised as she. her rough boots, her presence, wide shoulders, unflinching step. many asked her for directions. she studied the rolls of pavement, buckled with use, marvelled at the flick and gallop of traffic lights (the traffic absent, the light indignant red, gracious green). the crowd seemed to break and furrow around her. tight bundles of anger made knuckle-white hooked in her wake. aimlessness became a conversation. she spoke over the devil's voice, his intonations gathered in the depths of her throat, cupped in her palms. people sought after her, not following, but altering their path to come near, hear her calm. she glanced up at the devil a few times, called him an asshole when he said something stupid or talked as if he knew what he was saying. she wailed at his jokes, shook her fist and stomped the street. shouted hallelujah the few times he lapsed into silence. she knew he would jump, jump into the surge. she knew the dramatic possibilities, shivered.

lightning smacked. thunderheads gathered and low clouds collected the glare, arranged a frame for the devil up there amidst a swirling. solitary he teetered between the preposterous letters and the arms of the throng below. the drama amused him only as an afterthought. he shivered in the wind that stole the wet from his tongue. tremored his voice.

the devil spoke of horizons upon horizons. not of
rampage but of unhinging. eyes snapped open at his
suggestion. they cupped their hands to their mouths to shout
back up to him. they questioned him, asked his name.
encouraged him, hooted and jeered, debated with him.
perched four hundred feet in the air, the devil fell into
conversation. his podium contained no speech but words
flew, constructed a space between, around. out careened their
words, out of the glaring bold letters, out of the fires, the
release of sounds, hiss and roar, out of a green word, a
platform. the discussions with the devil grew. accents,
pitches, they shot into the night singing. at moments
incomprehensible. madness, babble of words. uncontained.

these then littered the street that night. the words
unhinged: anthem, escape, obsolete (spoken 'abslet' by a
mesmerizing singsong accent), bad (over and over this one,
in tongues the lips all touching to begin, b, the tongue letting
go, d, to nothing), whywhywhywhywhy, enuff, hey, pizza (a
practical chap in a greasy baseball cap – began a collection),
disruption, turnstiles that get stuck (we all hated that, knew
the surprising jerk-lurch back), lie, fear of (mail, male,
principals, principles, synonyms, slick black sedans, words,
words overtaking, losing), drinkh (the slur, a poem), lists,
listless, the letter, roaches, clerks, bottom lines, podiums,
marble walls (through rubber balls become endless), letting
go (this one, the devil's, 'just letting go' he said, the street so
far below), sister, hands, just simple hands (the old man's
gaze touched everyone's shoulder from behind), red skin not
so bad (as they warmed up to him), perhaps pandemonium
but the guy, an in'lectual by looking at him, was shushed,
scolded about them type of words, a radio blared reports of
the protest into the crowd, the account neat and accurate, the
bald owner of the corner store spat ended, that's us is it,
words to describe they were, turned off. inventing ears.

the crowd spoke as it never had before. in all history.
from the ragged edges trailing down Success, the hesitant

that bunched up by First National near the cops, the close press of loud jostling at the base of the Dominion. bodies milled and creased onto Ballad Ave., through Ardure St., frilled onto Power. plucked yield signs like fruit, a few pink leaflets were tucked into inside pockets as mementos. have you ever entertained the thought of me as your lover. directions presented themselves.

the night stretched into words, huge and smooth. Apology was there to catch it all.

but the words awaited use.

the devil leapt. swan.

Police Report – H757-A9366-67

September 14
Constable Stern
Sergeant Baryl

Myself and Constable Stern took the evidence collected on
Sept. 6 and analyzed for the location of printing. From a list
of seventeen presses we narrowed the location down to
three based on the paper type and print quality. These three
establishments were then approached. On Sept. 11, at one
location at 393 Cathedral Ave., Gilden and I discovered a few
remaining copies of the pamphlet. The manager of Bareback
Printing and Used Bookstore, Penny Carrier, informed us that
one of her employees had disappeared. It was an older
fellow she had employed only a few weeks previous. The
suspect went under the name Nick "Inkwell" Lithos. Carrier
informed us that he often slept at the printshop and didn't
think he had his own place. We took possible fingerprints
and they are being analyzed now. The name has turned up
blank and none of the other employees could offer much
information. They said he was eccentric but a fine worker.
They spoke fondly. Since he apparently did the printing late
one night, Carrier will not be charged. We have set up
surveillance. He left an abundance of traces but very few
leads. But with the description and the prints it should not be
long before we locate the accused.

Appearances: Photo #2
       huge gleaming wings his claws and horns edged with
a revenge-tale a dark red toothy grin flame and pitch smoke
broils over the orange glow of unleashed desire trickling over
his skin mocking assured eyes he looks by your gaze – you
have trouble looking away

friday, september 20

    he told me the history of dandelions, their yellow tenacity made strange. i never knew this but they came from europe. stowaway, they jumped ship and conquered a continent. isn't that amazing. the lowly dandelion. it works just as good as a buttercup to see if you like butter, or whether you're in love or not. the flower stalk is hollow and it hums if you spin it. the leaves are tender and juicy and go great in salads with sunflower seeds and apple chunks. the roots go forever. since columbus, or whoever, the dandelion's become a pest, a weed, reviled and scorned except by young girls who collect them by the armful for their mothers. some have taken it for what it is, tasted it, used it to make a tart wine, sharp and alive.

    the devil said his history is much the same. hold the devil underneath your chin to see if you're in love. his roots. forever and absurd. drunk on him.

    from now on, dandelions will always remind me of him.

"Alternate strains are to the
Muses dear."
—Virgil

I think it was the second time I had come out from the city. I had come through the barnyard from my car and up the back field, or pasture I guess it was. I was looking for signs of him picking my way through the cow pies. Not burnt grass or red pentagrams, I knew by then that these weren't the signs I needed. Walking by a meadow that dipped into the woods, saw Jay's herd standing around a cow and her dead calf. All the cows had their heads low and a deep moaning rumbled from their throats. They were mourning. The stupid things were actually mourning the dead calf. I looked at their hooves, their eyes and it didn't seem to match the idea of their sorrow. And then I saw Jay. There were tears in his eyes and I heard the higher strain of his mourning, his voice trailing above the cows'. I think it was then that I learned to love the man.

if   i   had

                    a   snowball's

          chance   if

a   snowball   had   if

          a   chance

                    i   had

          a   snowball

               if   chances

                         are

          i   would

                         if

sunday, september 27

*there just was no stopping him. one sweltering slow
afternoon he had come down from the attic where he had holed up
rummaging and digging. dust bloomed from his eyelashes as he
held up the pair of skates by their laces. the shape of a question. his
eyes widened as the words, the notion of blades iced into him. the
words – glide twist camel-spin double-axle toe-loop coast cut into
his mind. his body twitched with anticipation.*

freeze came surprisingly early that spring.

*on a sharp blue morning the devil donned his mitts and
laced up. he wobbled his way out across the newly frozen landscape.
crisp yellow grass whistled beneath his single-minded blades. no
snow had fallen yet and the dugout was a sparkling silver mirage in
the bleak fields.*

i told him the ice was thin.

yes he said

*he floated through the cattails his eyes on his blades and the
frayed white path that whined under his motion. he sailed in a wide
arc, his arms out catching the breeze, his breath left in white eddies
as he passed. he howled, he actually howled in what could only be
glee. he squealed pleasure.*

preacher man, look at me!

*he giggled and crowed as the ice groaned, snapped in his
wake. waves undulated, the ice rolling the stillness making the devil
a bright bobbing sun on the horizon. he jumped off the crests,
plunged into the troughs. the ice like cloth. like paper in the wind.
the devil sped on, twirling and weaving over the surface. his smile
broke the morning open.*

finally, with a sweet sucking noise, he fell through.

*without trace, the ice fell still. i struggled to catch sight of
him. "you! hey you! swim!" i vowed silently to find a name for him*

while i searched the heavy black waters, would the devil survive such a descent? there was no sign.

then i saw, right there at my feet. upside down he raced across the underside of the ice. feathery lines spread in the smooth secret surface. his blades nicked trailed screamed. when he came near i felt the ice shudder push against my feet. occasionally our feet met. bubbles bulged against the ice, splitting and popping in high keening bursts of laughter. he puffed his cheeks out as if holding his breath but i think that was just to make me feel better.

look at me &
he leapt

high

"This is not surprising, for worldly wisdom differs from divine just as plausibility differs from truth. While one is of heaven, the other is of earth; yet, according to the prince of matter himself, 'we know how to tell many lies that resemble the truth.' "
—Athenagoras

wednesday, september 28

in a lot of ways my mother and father were not my parents. both were absent, and then gone. all that i seem to have left are flashes of voices, phrases and saying. i cannot remember the shape of my mother's lips but yet i can hear her: 'could grow potatoes in them ears,' 'beats the heck outta me,' 'hold the phone,' 'catch you i can' (& me squealing, scampering away), 'fire it on out then' (when i stammered), 'jeeeezuz keeerist' (when i fell against the wood stove and knocked myself cold)

my dad called me 'spud' or 'jay-bird' had a peculiar way of saying 'real' with a long 'ulll' sound. all these sounds are echoes, bumps in the night.

today the devil asked me what it mean to be a 'real man' in a deep funny voice. i said, beats the heck outta me. beats the heck outta me.

"Langauage - n. The music with which we charm the serpents guarding another's treasure."
—Ambrose Bierce, *The Devil's Dictionary*

117

They came to know me as Chorus in town, got used to my snooping around, but nobody knew much about Jay or the devil. All they wanted to talk about was themselves and their neighbours, this feud or that complaint, and their odd rituals. I guess all small towns are like that but they sure do some strange things. Like the fall cattle drive right through the town when owners brought their herd back up from the leases. Buyers stood by and sent boys with buckets of bright paint to slop on choice flanks. Like the Friday Night Card Party. Like the annual women's broomball tournament that began in the Friesen's backyard rinks to show up a men's hockey tournament. The men soon lost interest and sulked while the women whooped it up. Like the post office soap box that was solely for the evaluation of the government because there was never time at the card parties. Like the ritual dumping of the Acorn Credit Union when the Bullneck boys hooked up their half-tons and tipped the converted granary on its side. Every year Mr. Smiley grew grey hairs on his grey hairs trying to resort the stacks of bills and stuff sent willy-nilly. The folk I ran into all loved to talk about anything if it meant an aside of scandal whispered with one hand held to the side of their mouth. Mrs. Sturgeon spoke every second sentence this way, leaning forward, her plump hand raised, tossing me tidbits and stories of lingerie and party lines.

When it came time to mentioning the devil there were just raised eyebrows, frowns, sidelong looks and abrupt goodbye's:

–tain't none in these parts fella
–got the wrong town son, devil don't got no place round here
–hell no, what would he do here, play cards? ha
–check Bluesky, they're a strange lot up there
–well, ol' Hedge been actin' mighty weird these days, but I don't reckon there be a demon in 'im

–sorry, partner, don't know the guy
–git lost, arsehole

When I brought up Jay they warmed up a bit, but I didn't get much to go on:

–oh, Jay, that feller still kickin'?
–don know much about 'im – holes up to hisself pretty much – quite a stutterer if i remember right
–hardworking boy – see 'im out on the fields afore anybody else – always makes 'is quota – hardworkin', hafta give 'im that – not a socializing guy tho, gits iz mail, sells iz cream and grain, buys iz tea and sugar, some hardware now and again, 'sbout it
–hardly know him, we shared a hospital bed together the year I had my stones taken out – they said it was bigger'n a baseball, tho I never saw the sucker, hurt like a sonofa . . . what was he in hospital for? hmmmmmm, I don't rightly know now that you mention it, he never said, never said much at all, jus' laid there, sometimes aworrin' 'bout the milkin', all bandaged up like a cocoon 'e was, his ears too, or was that his hands they was worryin' over – well he was in there for a good long time whatever it was. a good long time.

fear is a small time before winter – that was certain – it slid down the belly of hill down this side of the valley – the crops were in with the same kind of unfinished finality as always – an unfilfillment – this is the story of a winter departure – a retracing of new trails – the moon ticking – a winter's alarm stainless steel cold that beckons wet – tongue touch – fear is

tuesday, october 13

my diary has gone missing. when i woke up this morning and turned on my little bedside lamp it wasn't in its usual spot. instead, next to the aloe vera plant that sat on the old bible was a white paper lily that smelled like smoke. it rather threw my day off. a few months ago i would've instantly suspected the devil but this morning over oatmeal i just asked if he seen it around.

he said no, never noticed it, and offered to recite it back to me.

we laughed. it had kind of turned into a standing joke between us. i'd known for a long time that he read my diary. he often commented on the secrets that spilled into my writing. he soothed my fears, asked after El, poked and prodded at my inmost thoughts. i even found some minor edits, t's crossed, its changed to it's, some cumbersome adjectives stroked out, ungainly adverbs gone, words even lines scribbled out, digressions, explanations, funny rhymes spliced in, all in a careful script that looked very much like my own. i didn't mind. what could it hurt?

but who would steal someone's diary?

"– I am frightened of nothing in myself and you know nothing about me.
– Nothing? I know all that I have written about you.
– Who is speaking?"
—John Berger

"Magpie - n. A bird whose thievish disposition suggested to someone that it might be taught to talk."
—Ambrose Bierce, *The Devil's Dictionary*

The conversation turns. "You're Chorus. You made the devil go away." The accusation in her voice, but her body leaning, curious. The scrapbook still between us. I know I was guilty and the slender thread of trust we have is fraying. But there is something I still need to know. She speaks into my thoughts, holding my gaze, "He really is gone, you won't find him here." But that's not what I want. I think she is afraid of my obsession, my thoroughness. The devil had passed through my hands, and that was fine, but I needed to find one last thing, one last page. Catch gets up and walks to the door, puts on her jacket. The sun is almost setting but I follow her out into the woods, believing that she is considering forgiveness. Maybe I told too much, maybe I didn't show enough. I think it is time I forget my voice, let it go or learn it's accent, the way it catches the air, the way it inflects to end a sentence. question or.

sunday, october 21

he showed me where the coons sleep in the evergreens
where their dreams chuck pine cones loose. i showed him where a
moose had scraped off antlers last spring. he showed me where wild
pears still hung in wrinkles on the branch in a meadow of
solomon's seal and fescue, told me they go great in a rhubarb
chutney.

i showed him where a bear had turned stones looking for
grubs. he showed me how bulrushes explode when you whack them
against someone's belly, taught me the word hyssop.

i showed him whiskeyjacks, grackles, nuthatches, a purple
finch, and once a snowy owl swooped over our ears. he showed me a
beaver run in the new reeds, the mud slides, the tender poplar twigs
in hoarded bundles.

i showed him where rabbits had eaten bark, striped a stand
of trees as far as they could reach, so glaring white showed two feet
above the ground for miles. he showed me the strut and thump of
the prairie chicken, the grouse, the pleading thump he thought was
the greatest 'h' he had ever heard.

i showed him history in deer shit, the traces of my grain,
pin cherry pits, raspberry thorns and vetch. he showed me where
water had run into tiny cracks in an outcrop of granite and how it
had frozen the stone to pieces.

i showed him how i had hung a black paper silhouette of a
hawk in the front window so the sparrows and grosbeaks wouldn't
smack into the glass. how that without it they mistook the glass as
more sky or brush and dove thump into it. he showed me the bees,
the bees my father had left behind, the bees i couldn't keep. he
showed me their hive, their bodies bumping, their dance, their
intimate choreography from geography. he showed me that even
bees can lie as a scout relays places that don't exist just so he can
move closer to the queen. a dance of endless marigolds and daffodils
just to get the girl.

i showed him the hop of the magpie, its voice waiting for
words. he showed me moonlit snakeroot, delicate venus's slipper,
glowing stalks of enchanter's nightshade.

i showed him how coyotes send a decoy out by the east slough to lure Askim away from the chicken coop so they can raid, how they throw their high thin voices off the hillside to disorient. reading the forest we resisted going home, the night a crazy last page.

on a new moon, if you wrap four grains of wheat with a fresh clover leaf and hold it tight, you can see elves and goblins dance in the fiddleheads. the night a crazy last page.

as   razamataz; you spin and spell it out for me,
        abracadabra, a dabbling in the occult you find
        dazzling with dapper elixirs of jazzy sounding
        incantations you occupy covens with the blues of a
        completely different kind
if   once upon a time wasn't enough time at all what with
        all that treachery packed into one little moral, they
        had to invent a device to contain all that lechery, to
        invite you in for a lecture so they made up black
        magic back when narratology was new
as   apology and the devil eloped there developed a need,
        a precious need to make some magic; that neat
        miracle of seed, that immaculate conception of plot
        twist and birth of a brand new age; i would apologize
        but it is not for me to say what two reasonable
        responsible adults do in the privacy of their own
        canoe and can you blame me for contemplating the
        fiery consummation of such a consuming passion, a
        passion that questions, that brazenly displays itself,
        that could not help but make waves in such a
        ubiquitous pond
if   an imprint shifts away, the printer jostled just so, if
        the DNA has slipped, missed, caught against
        something, just past the mark so you cannot tell
        exactly what is   coming
as   magi, as magician, as wizard to a thousand kings the
        devil knows the magic of touch, the puffs of smoke
        and faint sleight of hand, breaks the rules of spelling
        that deal us into someone else's hands a slight weight
        in your hand
if   a pregnant pause waits for security then his silence
        becomes a testament to history
as   the devil pranced and glowed he would put a hand
        on my belly, my scar kicking against me, due
if   when you wish upon a star you tell someone else it
        won't come true; just keep it to your self, is that what

they're saying don't expose yourself to the outer
atmosphere is that what they're saying
as   if; if 'as if' were enough; worth naming a star after;
worth waiting to tell when it's the perfect time; worth
talking yourself into

if

the rimrocks stand, a testament to fear

scraping the edge of panic

the sky fell, sounding hollow

a falling star (didja?)

a bomb, the forest fell (didja hear?)

the name of flame, a wind-walker

ground shaking like knees

the dirt pushed up, waved

away to stone, quick landing

medusa's eyes of diamond glint

horseshoe-luck, tossed topography

 a spread of stone hands

waiting to catch your breath

up into windlessness, like surprise

a lone eye blinking on the edge

fear a brink of falling into

the devil answered, yes

the devil's last poem

t   ng
t   ng
t   ng
t   ng
t ng   tng

ooooooooooooooooooooooooooooh

tng

ssshhhhhhhhhhhhhhhhhhhhhhhhh
pssst
pssssssssst
ssshhhh   tng

                                    ooh
tng   i
tng   sssssss
i   sssssss
i   sssssssssssssss
i   sssss
i sss
tng   ice
tsh   haaaah

127

he stood on the hill top looking at you while i slept.
absolutely still. he said he was dying through the set of his
shoulders the glaze over his eyes. and that he was afraid. and
sad. he said many things, told stories, old stories with
strange spirits and motions. recounting. the rehearsed,
considered. his voice began. wavers. waves as altered tone, a
cadence shifting phrases that flashed on his tongue. wet
alfalfa flowers. like blackberry seeds. like tongue-blood after
a fall. he told you his burden. the weight of his damn tail, his
red, blaring a shame not his own, his flame, his difference
like a pyre, his pride, and his need, absence made fantastic,
his gravity, pulling him, pulling you after. he exorcised
words. worried over them like seedlings. long fervent
speeches with stakes at either end. low scandalous whispers
dripping with fruit. terrified denials. tirades. proclamations
bloomed. manifestoes, succulent and smooth. in greek. in
arabic. hebrew. latin. german they flew from him as if
released under pressure. shit, he murmured. mumbled into
himself. his eyes on your he vomited. spontaneous. opened
up. gushed. fire bone fruit feathers scales chains robes
stained glass candles vials scrolls snakes earthquakes girdles
two pitchforks a murder of crows a black sedan with tinted
windows dice dimes brimstone hemlock caviar neon
telephones a handful of crocus petals stars with telescopes
attached a silencer crowns toads toxic waste barbed wire
bats' wings inkwells sulphur dioxide. he released emptied.
purged. he said he was dying. you lose him in the motion.
the violence of his expulsion. you mourn. come back to wake
me. tell me what you saw.

They say the Friday Night Card Party at Baytree Town Hall used to actually take place on Friday night. One hot summer long ago, every Friday always turned out to be clear days and the tractors and combines worked late. They say it was such a good year that there were bumper crops, third and even fourth cuts of hay, granaries strained at the seams, and farmers worked by moonlight to get all that into market and haysheds. Saturdays that year always seemed to be rainy so the Friday Night Card Party came to fall on Saturday and since then always has.

This suited Scoop just fine. Scoop is the town drunkard and official layabout. Friday would have been difficult for Scoop. He is paid by Mrs. Sturgeon to do odd jobs, usually of a mechanical nature in which Scoop showed flashes of brilliance but also includes chauffeuring her and her pristine daughter around and spying on the neighbours. His Friday paycheck is instantly translated into a roaring drunk that climaxes with everything from a virtuoso serenade of the Chisum's Hereford bull to a legendary encounter with Mrs. Sturgeon in which he reportedly jiggled her jowls and promptly mooned her and her wide-eyed daughter.

By Saturday he usually recovered and had smoothed any ruffled feathers. He opened the hall and fired up the old wood stove, shooing mice away as he shuffled around. Patting his belly and crowing to himself he set the tables in a wide circle. Now for some real drinking.

Almost everyone in Baytree came to the Friday Night Card Party. Jay, El, and Apology were viewed as eccentric because of their absence. Children shouted and dodged underfoot and old codgers sat regally in corners. They came not so much for the cards as for the opportunity to argue. Massive amounts of talk and liquor made up the card party. It served as town council meeting without wasting time for an actual 'meeting,' a word that evoked a chorus of spitting and under-the-breath 'jeeezus's' at the best of times. Nobody could rightly remember who the town councillors were. The debates that floated haphazardly around the tables were legendary. Momentous decisions came into being: the Great Swindle-Stall Landclaim Dispute (eight acres of prime creek-bed was awarded to the victorious Stall clan), the Great Yellow Grater Purchase, and, who could forget, the Landmark Disbandment of Wednesday Night Town Council Meetings. At the card party no discussion could run between tables, and argument was passed bit by bit as the winning hands moved clockwise, the others counter. Only Mrs. Sturgeon was allowed to sit stationary near the stove because of her rheumatism (the Great Sturgeon Landing Rule, they said). The card game is trump whist and the subtleties of play are a time-honoured tradition in Baytree. With the issues came an intricate code of card protocol. Protocol that is as old as Baytree itself, or so they say.

El & Jay sat across from each other
the cards fell in dizzying patterns
already always
& the game
was lost
to them

Washing dishes one evening the devil, elbow deep in mugs and butter knives, looked sidelong at Jay:

– ready for the big card party tonight
– there's a card party every week, why would this one be big
– because you're finally going to one
– ya, i was thinking about it – i-i thought, well, i . . .

The devil, being sympathetic to the subtle pathways of desire, clued into the tender places love opens, the shy risk of lust, the careful give and take of courtship, the tentative balance between restraint and hint, as always, talked a gentle persuasion, hooked roundabout into the red suspenders of love:

– of course you're going, El'll be there, and I know you're hot for her – watcha gonna wear?

Suds flew. Jay was hustled in front of a mirror, hair fussed over, jackets and socks matched. The devil grinned, finally, admiring his dashing creation. He leaned close.

– you got a safe?
– a safe? i have nothing valuable enough for a safe.
– oh, yes you do. no i mean a rubber, you know, a glove . . . no you don't, do you, okay, okay, here – pretend this is a raincoat, when it gets wet . . .

The devil tucked the package into Jay's shirt, chucked him under the chin, jogged his shoulder, had him by the lapels.

– now go out there & make me proud, son

sunday, november 4

    they never said anything about dancing
    *the Friday Night card party had a dance. the devil led us
into line, all the women across from the men. the two lines faced
each other. they just stood there. Glen Miller i think it was. bold
and ringing with resolve. people called along the lines, jokes about
boots and beards. the women tossed a few barbs across at the men,
their hands on their hips, secretly rejoicing in the company of other
women, shoulder to shoulder. Apology leaned against a beam, her
tongue in her cheek, listening to the banter. she wore a black
body-suit, grey wool socks and a red scarf. eyebrows edged up as
she passed, her body causing stirs, altering conversations. El had
arrived late, clomping through the door with big kodiak boots still
steaming with cowshit. she mumbled something about a bloated
heifer. she wore a bulky black sweater and her big toe poked out of
one sock. it was a wonderfully shaped toe. she settled near Apology
and finally looked at me. her little smile made my body shudder, my
breath caught, my belly muscles tightened, my feet tingled.*
    *i wondered about love. was love a skill, like engine repair or
art, or like learning to do a trick, a dangerous trick with blades or
fire? does it take practice? is the first time like trying to juggle for
the first time, oranges thumping into the linoleum, rolling under
the stove? i felt on the verge of heroic. i wondered at love, there in
that line of men, and then the devil broke away.*
    *he moved away from the men still chatting about diesel or
something. some said afterward that he was on his way to the
outhouse, some claimed he was on his way across to the women,
still others thought he was slowly beginning to dance on his own, a
quick step, spin, and . . . regardless, there, in the middle of the
dance floor, the devil stumbled, twisted like smoke, gravity hot
against his feet, fell hard, his head bouncing against the planks,
hands slapping the floor like a hockey player's stick, looking for a
penalty.*
    *conversation stopped. the lines stood. the figure of the devil
crumpled into an impossible heap in their midst. he, for an instant,
was the most alone thing in the universe.*
    we rushed to him. rushed like dogs. rushed like barley when

that sweet west wind comes across the foothills with the faint smell of salt. rushed like children at recess. headlong, careening, jostling to pick him up. a hundred hands at once touched him, winched him up.

> *— i'm okay, it's okay, i just hurt my heel.*
> *— ya, you just wanta get outta dancin with me.*

Apology towered over him, arms crossed. she threw him over her shoulder, began to sway to the shrill of trumpet, the jaw of trombone. bodies found bodies next, jostle turned to an awkward step, a tentative lean and twist. with whoever, happen-stance, whichever. neighbours, wives, neighbouring daughters, customers, employees, young and old. they all danced, breaking step only to switch partners. i was spun into El, into her words, her question, is windlessness a word. i didn't think so.

here's the deal

the last hand, a crowd gathers to watch

a no trump hand, the lead: Mrs. Sturgeon, eight of hearts, a
fleshy shrug, she glares over at the devil across from her, he
is still arranging his cards, shuffling, rearranging continually.

the devil: jack of hearts, notices her glare, sips his cream
soda, stares at the cards harder, leads: the ace of hearts, no,
pulls it back, plays it anyway.

Sturgeon: gasps, queen of hearts, she has a slice of
poundcake, a folding fan and a huge tumbler of grapefruit
juice and rye, taps impatiently.

the devil: three of clubs, grins at Sturgeon, sips.

Sturgeon: king of clubs, loses under the ace, she humphs,
pulls on her left ear, glares at the devil, the room is silent.

the devil: follows the ten of spades with the queen, pulls on
his nose, glares at Sturgeon. Sturgeon: nine of spades, king
follows, grips her cards tight folding them slightly, turns a
darker shade of red, rubs her shoulder.

the devil: follows with . . . hesitates, looks at Sturgeon . . . a
king of hearts over a seven, he leans over the table, "ummm
. . . what are we playing for here, if you don't mind me
asking," a young girl pokes his arm and points to three
rhubarb pies on a far table, the devil's eyes bug, he licks his
lips, concentrates on his cards hard.

Sturgeon: six of hearts, sighs, gulps, dribbles, leans forward
with a look that forces a murmur from the crowd.

the devil: looks at Sturgeon, grabs a card at random, mouths 'what?,' nine of diamonds. Sturgeon: raises her eyes, slaps the ten down in disgust, snaps her fan open, leads the eight of spades, the table shuddering with her impatience.

the devil: scratches his armpits, looks up, studies his cards, winces, finger on chin, looks up, shifts in his chair, touches a card, pulls back, hisses, pulls another, offers it with both hands, the ace of diamonds.

Sturgeon: kicks under the table . . .

the devil: tosses cards, table, drinks into the air, runs for cover, hearts spin, clubs plummet, diamonds skitter across the floor, chairs clatter and fold, the devil is yelling 'what?' over and over, Sturgeon is bellowing for help overturned like a turtle, the seven of hearts tucked into her hair-bun, the devil disappears between dancing feet.

A SNAKE UNDER OUR TREE!

Rumour has abounded. Today, Baytree residents are buzzing over rampant word that a demon has been let loose on our town. An official from the City, who has asked to remain anonymous, has been interviewing townspeople concerning the strange sightings. Many reports have come in but it is difficult to make any sense of the conflicting accounts. The unnamed official has been quoted as saying "everything is under control" but refused to comment further.

First word of the demon came because of a telephone misconnection in which poor Bula Bellows found herself chatting with a minion of the underworld. Imagine her surprise! She is quoted as saying, "he was impertinent, rude, and made disgusting noises." Since then there have been numerous reports of a "mean little shadowy man" running naked through town after midnight. Local dogs and geese have been in a frenzy. Clothes, especially women's underwear, have gone missing from clotheslines everywhere. Some even claim the disruption at the Friday Night Card Party was due to the devil. Mrs. Sturgeon: "It was him all right . . . the little _____ should be shot!"

So far, no culprit has been found.

At the hospital in Bonanza, the doctors had never met Jay but an old nurse remembered him. She stopped her bustling around and stood with a clipboard held against her chest. She put her glasses on and off, on and off again as she talked:

– Oh, yes, I remember Jay the poor fella – came in on the coldest night i ever saw – musta been round -45, wind like you wouldn't believe – windows cracked at the cold, horses died, milk was freezin' in the udder, I swear – he came in for frostbite and, worse yet, bad bad burns on his chest and tummy – nasty stuff it was treatin' both those at once – Justin Peachy brought him in, said they found him on their step half-frozed, clutchin' his belly and mumbling about the chores and nonsense – he took forever to recover – and his scars, i remember my eyes gettin' lost in them scars – found out later his parents were killed in the fire – just like that.

Jay found himself becoming more of a night person, straying freely beyond sunset. The devil lurked there, and one night Jay found him on the porch looking at the stars. His gaze travelled across them, his neck bobbing like he was studying cave drawings, galloping buffalo, stick figures, hand prints in relief. His hands twitched as if straining to rearrange, alter the constellations.

Jay rarely saw the stars, and if he did, it was the last few at dawn. The bright startled him and he saw for the first time shadows cast by starlight.

He moved next to the devil.

– watching the heavens, eh?

There was a long silence. The devil slumped a little where he stood. He looked down to the ground, sighed long, sighed for minutes, like it was his last. His breath smelled like cucumber.

– no . . . no, not the heavens, those are stars, suns a long long way away.
– i know that, it's j-just an expression.

– they're far too beautiful for heaven. there is a history up there. heaven is too easy. there are too many names up there to lump into heaven. heroic Cepheus and Perseus surrounding poor Cassiopeia, stapled there to that throne. Hercules, Ophiuchus, Orion in those damnable poses. the Bears, the Dogs, the Swan, the Serpent, the Dragon. Draco curling there, filling half the sky. chaos isn't it. and those star names, those star names sounding like sand against rock, like the dry rasp of lips, cloth against bone. Kochab, Dubhe, Rushbah, Yildun, Procyon (that one there, just near the horizon), Merak, Scheat, Tejat, El Kophrah, Pherkad. does that sound like heaven to you. you cannot dispel pain so easily. the maps, the sounds, they do not lie. Mirach, Sulufat, Azelfafage, Zaurak. they do not lie. they are the scars on the belly of your heaven. say their names with me. Sabik, Thuban, Ras Algethi, Phecda, Asif, Alya. pain is a step away from hate, share my thirst.

Jay was sucked into the sadness of that voice, the sentence filtering from lips like water. There was a flash, a streak of light penciled across the northern sky over the pines.

     – i know, it's not a falling star, it's a meteor falling through the air.

     – didja make a wish?
     – yes

 They looked up again. A shower of northern lights crackled green-white and purple onto the sky. The promise of ice on your tongue, they slid down to just above your face. The devil whispered.

     – if you whistle, you can make the lights dance, and if you whistle loud and well, it drips onto your tongue

Our lips moved to move the sky.

mmmmmmmmmmmmmmmmmmmmmmmmmmmmmmmmmm

saturday, december 3

>*chorus came to the door. it was time it seemed.*
>*the devil touched my shoulder. this is what he said before he*
left me.

>*– eventually, he is going to catch up to me, but not now. it*
would ruin my grand exit wouldn't you say. no, no, don't look at
me like that. i could disappear in a giant rush of flames and smoke –
i could – after all that's what they would want. but i'm not. i won't.
no miracles. you must look through me, preacher man. look at me
now and look through me. horizon is plural and begins with
nothing. nothing but the great perhaps i go to. (he stopped) but who
am i saying goodbye to?
>*– maybe me.*
>*– then meet me by the skating dugout at dawn.*

>*he ran through the kitchen and leapt out the back window*
with a strange fire in his eyes just as chorus clicked open the front
door asking if anyone was home. hello . . .

– Hi, you are Jay no doubt. Call me Chorus. Could I have a word with you . . . if it would be no trouble.

– No, no. Yes of course. Come in. Let me t-t-take your coat fore the dog gits all over it.

– Yes, and what's your name, furry guy?

– Askim.

– Ask him?

– That's his name, Askim. I'll be right back . . . make yourself . . . Askim git down . . . at home.

Jay left him behind in the living room and went into the kitchen more to think than anything else. There, he shuffled through cupboards for something to offer the stranger while he ran through guesses at who he was.

(okay – the mortgage is behind but not as much as it has been and his suit doesn't look like a banker's really so . . . letsee, graham crackers? no those are for kids – is there an election coming up? i don't think so and he hasn't given me any pamphlets or anything – buns, we got buns, and that corned beef i was trying to use up - he can't be a cop or he would have said so right away – orange juice or tea, no, doesn't look like a tea-guy, got some coffee somwhere – oh, jesus, maybe someone's died – but who, i don't know anybody, really – oooooo, walnuts, that'll do it – on no, maybe he's some religious-type, and i just sat him down – he'll be here forever and i've got work to do – oh well, might as well face the music. . . . shi . . .)

–. . . t, p-p-pardon me, I lost a bun at the d-d-door there, I'll be right back.

(ya, ya, here ya go Askim – he has a fake smile and what is he doing poking in my books?)

– S-Sorry about that, I didn't mean to l-leave you hanging, I'm not used to having g-g-guests.

– Not at all. Thank you for having me Jay . . . can I call you Jay? That's all everyone called you in town & I don't know your last name.

– Jay's fine just fine. Nuts?

– No thank you. Jay, I came to see you because I am looking for something I think you might know something about.

– Something?

Chorus is sitting at the end of the couch, the window is behind making his face difficult to see. He has set a file folder on the end table where the devil has rested his feet the night before. Jay is sitting on the edge of his chair, elbows on his knees, hands clasped in front of him. Chorus has leaned backward and spread his arms across the back of the couch. He occasionally cocks his head as if listening for something, the way a dog listens for mice under the floorboards.

– Jay, I am a sort of reporter and I'm looking for something very unusual. In fact you probably won't believe me when I tell you . . . unless, well, unless . . . I am hunting a dangerous . . . man who has a . . . unique appearance. You couldn't miss him. First of all, he, well, he has a tail. . . .

– Umm, the coffee is ready, back in a b-b-bit

He kept walking through the kitchen, ducked out the back window, ran to El's.

Wait . . . did you hear that?

142

ladies and gentlemen, hobos and tramps
four-legged spiders and three-legged aunts
the admission is free so pay at the door
pull up a chair and flop on the floor
one fine day in the middle of the night
two dead men got up for a fight
back to back they faced each other
drew their swords and shot one another
the deaf policeman heard the din
and came to rescue the two dead men
if you don't believe this lie I sing
ask the blind guy, he saw everything

I saw a few titles on his bookshelf. They all seemed
unfamiliar but I can remember a few I think. There was one
called Alibi, A Fixed Address, a music book called The Heart
of Thinking or something, Bloody Jack, Gargantuan, a history
of William Bonney, Headframe, one about Noah's ark, the
Magic of Herbs, Cinders, Mother Earth News, Alice in
Wonderland (I thought that was for kids), House of Fame,
Martyrology, If on a Winter's Night a Traveller (although
pieces of that one seemed to have fallen out), Birdman, the
Farmer's Almanac, and some old ones, Dante, Anthony
Bierce, Milton, but most were obscure and looked like they
weren't very interesting stories. Too much poetry. He had
some records too. Louis Armstrong, Buddy Bolden, Hank
Williams, Hoagie Carmichael, Billy Holiday, a few others.
They didn't look like they were in very good shape, warped
by heat, and I didn't see a record player. His collection
surprised me though, I didn't expect him to be interested in
art. I thought all he cared about were those cows.

                books lifted off
              helium filled words
        rustled and shushed through the room
                    swooped around the chorus
            flicked off curtains and ears
              slipped by with a quick

            paper cut cheek

the rimrocks
like teeth beneath a grin or a kiss

like forgiveness, the residue of memory, told again

like the footprint of a giant, unrecognizable from down here

like a sieve, catching through liquid rush, cool and cleansing

like love, you wondering, alone

like sin, free, fallen, one step too far

like excess, spilling, stains the neat prairie starch

like a horseshoe for luck, pointing up, discoloured by clay

like embrace, release and possession

like a secret, too big to keep, too sprawling to share

like a scar, shrinking over time, erosion let go

like a break in the horizon, snagging your stutter

like whirlwind, air isolated, poetry, curling in

like a collection, hands out, palms up, catching you, sudden

saturday, december 4

    this was the last i would see of the devil. i found him standing alone at the rimrocks.

    he held a chunk of ice in both hands. the plains and crevices pearled with water trickling trailing down edges. wet light with a slick clicking sound.

    he stared amazed. "you can see the other side." he traced his fingers over the opposite face. "you can see everything." he turned the ice gasping at the play of sun. drops wetted his arms his shins his appetite. he smiled at the excess flapping at his senses.

    something flashed into his thought, crystalised with long rainbow streaks feathery at the ends. his head snapped around toward me as if, as if he had not know my plain linger at his side. his cool gaze quick-froze into mine. i paled tried to slip away.

    preacher man, preacher man – turn me into ice!

        begin by turning me into ice
            & there was storm

       and when i turned
          his name
    still   sound
        caught in the quick
            catch of cold

      i found him
          gone

(preacher man, it's snowing
         snowing to beat hell!)

And for the first time, I see the Rimrocks. She leads me to the edge. I remember windlessness, look down. Turning to Catch, I find her close and she reaches out, touches my neck, as only Catch can. "You're Chorus again, now I think I know you, I know you." She walks away and begins to tell me about that burning cold night. Tells me that Jay's parents were killed in the burning house, how they re-entered to find him, the frantic search through the house, the furniture, the familiar hallways shattering, how his mother plucked him out of the flames while she burned, blind, engulfed with fire, she threw him over her shoulder, tossed him out a back window, and then was lost. "While she burned," she gives me the words, throws them to me as we walked. Not out of any sense of duty, or debt, just to make it come together, meet, like hands on the other side of an embrace. The sun set, a light scar behind my eyes. The horizon is a mouth. We begin to walk again beneath the stars. Perfect and unsure. Bundles of energy and breath hhhhhhhhhhhhhhhhhhhhhhhhh breathing

Recent titles from Turnstone Press

Lunar Wake
poetry by Catherine Hunter

Girl by the Water
poetry by Gary Geddes

Blasphemer's Wheel
Selected and New Poetry by Patrick Friesen

Dorothy Livesay's Poetics of Desire
criticism by Nadine McInnis

Jiggers
poetry by Todd Bruce

Falling in Place
poetry by Patrick O'Connell

A Fine Grammar of Bones
poetry and prose by Méira Cook